Facilitating Organisational Change within Development Organisations

About the author

Fons van der Velden is a social entrepreneur, founder and non-executive director of Context, international cooperation (Utrecht, the Netherlands) and Foresee Social Entrepreneurs Pvt Ltd (Bangalore, India). These two companies provide (business development) support to social entrepreneurs and development organisations, which may vary from strategic positioning, to hands-on support and conceptualisation and theorising.

He has done extensive action research in India and countries in sub-Sahara Africa. He has a long track record as a trainer, facilitator and researcher. He has published extensively about foreign aid, international division of labour, the concepts of social business and organisational learning including *Regional development and the international division of labour* and *Private development aid in transition*, both published by Concept Publishing Company.

Prior to founding Context, international cooperation, Fons van der Velden worked at the Centre for International Development Issues Nijmegen (University of Nijmegen) where he continues as a guest faculty. http://www.linkedin.com/in/fvdvelden

Facilitating Organisational Change within Development Organisations

A Resource Book for Development Practitioners

Edited by

Fons van der Velden

CONCEPT PUBLISHING COMPANY PVT. LTD., NEW DELHI-110059

ISBN-13: 978-81-8069-991-7

First Published 2013

Published and Printed by

Concept
Since 1974

Concept Publishing Company Pvt. Ltd.
A/15-16, Commercial Block, Mohan Garden
New Delhi-110059 (India)
T: 25351460, 25351794, *F*: 091-11-25357109
E: publishing@conceptpub.com, W: www.conceptpub.com
Editorial Office: H-13, Bali Nagar, New Delhi-110 015, India.

Cataloging in Publication Data--Courtesy: D.K. Agencies (P) Ltd. <docinfo@dkagencies.com>

Facilitating organisational change within development organisations : a resource book for development practitioners / edited by Fons van der Velden.
p. cm.
Includes bibliographical references (p.) and index.
ISBN 9788180699917

1. Organizational change. 2. Economic development. 3. Industrial capacity. I. Velden, Fons van der.

DDC 658.406 23

Dedication

This book is dedicated to my small big friend
Abdul Shakur Eillyas,
that he may have the opportunity to develop his talents.

Motto

'Capabilities belong first and foremost to individual persons, and only derivatively to groups'

Martha Nussbaum, 2011

Foreword

The only thing that is constant is change.
Heraclitus, Greek Philosopher, 500 BC

As thinking-learning beings, the remarkable evolution of the human is always a source of much research and exploration. Developments and modifications in the world - be it in technology or in our mindsets - are highly fast paced now, more than ever. To deal and engage with them to best suit the needs and interests of the constituencies concerned, becomes an onerous task for those who seek to bridge the gaps in these transformative processes. If individuals are grappling with persistent change, can organisations be far behind?

The nature of development work is subject to revision and adaptation in a fast-evolving development paradigm that has at present much to consider: a crisis in the Eurozone, shrinking of development aid, emerging concerns relating to climate change and the ever-widening gap between the rich and the poor. Changing times mandate a change in approaches. Organisations, like people need to evolve and step up to adapt to these variations. It is in this light that the focus on Capacity Development becomes essential. A book chronicling some of the best practices and the experiences of change processes within development organisations would guide organisations and practitioners in realising what they can expect and what could be possible strategies to align and cope with the changes. This is the attempt the book intends to make.

Development agencies have multiple priorities: they have to serve reference communities and handle donor requirements and keep them in line with their existing vision and mission and at the same time ensure that their systems (strategy, administration, human resources, finance and legal matters) are updated and well-functioning. Capacity development is not just related to programmatic interventions, but also has a bearing as regards making the necessary micro-macro linkages and looking at outcomes and impacts that match with the goals and aspirations of the constituencies the development agency engages with. In a nutshell, capacity development in this context is about making the far-sighted, long-term investment in the right people and enhancing their knowledge, skill sets and motivation to help them commit to processes that can help direct and facilitate better, the lives of the communities and groups they work with. The best mélange of interventions, strategies, structures and systems would be an outcome of the dynamic efforts an organisation would undertake and in the endeavours they would make to be relevant and sustainable in the prevailing context.

The book reflects among others on how Non-Governmental Development Organisations such as Cecoedecon, whose experiences have been highlighted in this book, have demystified an organisational change process. As chairperson of the organisation, I have had the opportunity to be part of some of the processes, e.g., the board retreat. I have observed over a period of three years the serious, systematic and rigorous engagement the organisation had with change strategies and the learning and growth trajectory the process effected. What is important is that although serious and systematic, the process was also very comfortable and almost like a celebration of collective learning. At no point was it pressurising for the stakeholders involved – the staff, community, other allied civil society organisations, the board, academics, legal fraternity and media.

The approach has been unique with the involvement of multiple stakeholders to ensure that the process was dynamic, engaging, constant and progressive. The well-struck balance between the academic considerations of Organisational and Institutional Development and consolidating and strengthening capacities through the process that was undertaken is noteworthy.

It is not always the Darwinian principle of the survival of the fittest that is at play. Development organisations especially those which function like a family unit, such as Cecoedecon, value all its members and contributors and 'doing away' with those not in tandem with the changing context, is not the first route they would adopt. Instead, enriching and diversifying the capacities of existing staff and making room for a more enabling working environment and taking everyone collectively forward, is what this process has been about. This is a page that other similar development organisations, can definitely take from this book.

Meant as a handy ready-reckoner to understand Capacity Development, the book is an effort by reflective development practitioners who have tried to weave in a multiplicity of factors from grassroots experiences, policy analysis, role of state and civil society as a whole and the dilemmas therein. Aimed to leave the reader with some valuable lessons and an initiation to look creatively at strengthening communities and development agencies, the book seeks to be a catalyst in paving the way for a more effective and relevant development practice.

January, 2013
Jaipur (India)

Justice V.S. Dave (Retd.)
Chairperson, Cecoedecon
President, Association of Retired Judges of Supreme Court and High Courts of India

Contents

List of Major Abbreviations

CBO	Community Based Organisation
CD	Capacity Development
CDC	Civic Driven Change
Cecoedecon	Centre for Community Economics and Development Consultants Society
CRG	Consulting Role Grid
ECDPM	European Centre for Development Policy Management
FGD	Focused Group Discussion
HRD	Human Resource Development
ID	Institutional Development
IOB	Policy and Operations Department of the Dutch Ministry of Foreign Affairs
KSSM	Kisan Seva Samiti Mahasangh (farmers union)
LFA	Logical Framework Approach
LSP	Listening, Summarising and Probing
MDGs	Millennium Development Goals
MTR	Mid-Term Review
OD	Organisational Development
PIIRD	Participatory Initiatives for Integrated Rural Development
SD	Systems Development
SRoI	Social Return on Investment
ToT	Training of Trainers
UNDP	United Nations Development Programme

Introduction

Fons van der Velden[1]

Introduction: from personnel service to capacity development

The role of civil society in the development discourse has become more and more pertinent in recent debate. In efforts to improve aid effectiveness[2], not only the role, but also the challenging task of strengthening civil society has been the subject of much discussion on the development agenda. Within the broad spectrum of discussions, a particular interest in capacity development (CD) has emerged in recent years. This trend is evident from capacity development studies[3] which have been commissioned by the Dutch and Belgium government, Partos (the umbrella organisation of NGDOs in the Netherlands) and by various international publications about CD.[4]

Capacity development is 'hot' and high on the agenda of development agencies. In efforts to address social, economic and environmental issues, the importance of improved competencies, collective capabilities and capacity[5] have become ever more evident. This has led to the emergence of CD as a dominant and defining approach.

Over the past three decades capacity development has slowly but steadily emerged from personnel service overseas (expatriate personnel available in situations of absolute or relative shortage of qualified personnel in low and medium income countries for local development organisations[6]); Technical Assistance (broadening the scope to more than just personnel assistance), to capacity development.

What is capacity development?

In accordance with the definitions that have been formulated by the United Nations Development Programme (UNDP)[7]:

> *Capacity* is defined as 'the ability of people, organisations, and society as a whole to manage their affairs successfully'.
> *Capacity Development* is the process whereby people, organisations and society as a whole unleash, strengthen, create, adapt, and maintain capacity over time.
> *Capacity Development Support* is the process that contributes the resources, the strategies, the motivations and the ideas to encourage the development or emergence of abilities.

In other words 'capacity something' is about the energy, drive of people, organisations and institutions to take responsibility for the way they function and their contribution to society at large. Capacity development is not a neutral nor a technical issue, it is, as will be described in this book, about socio-political change and a shift in power equations at personal, organisational and institutional level.

The generic definitions surrounding CD should be treated with a word of caution. In order to gain a deeper and appropriate meaning, *Capacity*, *Capacity Development* and *Capacity Development Support* are concepts and approaches that need to be understood from within a specified socio-political and cultural context. A 'one size fits all' approach will not suffice.

Core messages of the present volume

This book has emerged from interaction with development practitioners, policy makers, social entrepreneurs and academics through trainings, learning trajectories, evaluations and action research. The core ambition behind its development is to provide an introduction, a primer, into the subject of CD.

The following six areas of research are a reflection of the main message and content of this book.

Images of 'organisations'

The approach taken toward Capacity, Capacity Development and Capacity Development Support is highly determined by the way in which one defines and understands the ins and outs of an 'organisation' (the image). Some — in the tradition of Frederick Taylor — still perceive organisations as machines that can be engineered quite easily from outside ("Taylorism'); or state that 'there is nothing inside organisations only cost'[8]. At the other end of the spectrum some perceive organisations as rather fluid, living entities, such as Taylor from the CDRA: 'My sense is that people see organisations as a vehicle through which to do things in the world, not realising that in building organisations they are shaping the world'[9] and the former CDRA Director Kaplan who goes on to define organisations as social organisms whereby it is important to understand and master the invisible dimensions.[10] This is not just pseudo-intellectual hair-splitting but an observation with substantial implications for approaches to capacity development support. The different ways in which one perceives organisations leads to entirely different approaches to CD and change management in general.

A highly personal issue

For the longest time now, CD in the aid sector has been viewed with an eye of contempt by Northern NGDOs and development practitioners. CD is something which was boxed together with communities, community based organisations, partner organisations and Southern NGDOs, but not 'about us' Northern agencies and certainly not 'us' as development practitioners.

This view is, however, changing substantially; more and more studies indicate that CD is first and foremost a highly personal issue. CD is about an 'individual's attitudes, values, styles and resulting priorities and actions (or inertia) are often a break or make point'.[11]

Martha Nussbaum writes: 'Capabilities belong first and foremost to individual persons, and only derivatively to groups. The approach espouses a principle of *each person as an end*'.[12] Such an approach stipulates that the goal is to enhance capacity for each and every person and 'not to use some people as a means to the capabilities of others or of the whole'.[13] Such a focus on a person makes a huge difference for policy, strategy and the practice of CD in which a clear link will need to be established between the individual and the collective (team, department, and organisation) capabilities.[14]

Indivisibility of capacity development

The insight that capacity is a highly personal issue should be combined with the observation that — in view of the organic inter-relatedness of organisations and individuals, the multiplicity of actors that are involved in CD and the phenomenon of co-creation—capacity development cannot be understood as an isolated phenomenon. It is intrinsically linked to the idea of the existence of 'others'. Consequently, CD is indivisible in terms of actors, capabilities and processes. Each actor needs the others in order to change its own capacity. In other words, the capability of one actor cannot be enhanced without a corresponding change taking place within the other. This requires CD to foster mutuality and reciprocity. For instance, the process of CD does not take place only in the domain of the Southern partner organisations; it also takes place in the donor's domain.

Summing up, the capacity of 'them' is also the capacity of 'us'. Efforts to capture and nurture this indivisible nature of CD calls for thorough approaches and tools when it comes to policy and planning, as well as monitoring and evaluation.[15]

Capacity development is about power

In recent times, CD has become known to many as a 'process developing from within and driven by individuals, organisations and (systems within) societies; these processes and their outcomes are influenced by power dynamics within the system and its context'.[16] Working in constant collaboration with others, involves a high variety of challenges, particularly in the areas of giving and taking power.[17]

It has to be acknowledged that even in a context of common concern and mutual respect, the issue of power continues to play an important role, both implicitly and explicitly. For instance the power dynamics of North-South relationships need to be recognised as an aspect of the relational processes and needs to be managed in a CD process accordingly.

Intricacies at operational level: the value of long term relationships

In the early 1990's UNDP led an in-depth review of the role of *Technical Cooperation*, which resulted in the so called 'Berg Report'.[18] The report concluded that technical cooperation had proven effective in getting the job done, but was found to be less effective in efforts to develop local institutions or strengthen local capacities. This was due to the fact that technical cooperation was expensive, supply and a donor-driven approach led to limited local ownership, which often heightened the dependence on foreign experts and distorted the local labour market. The report called for 'radical changes', including the greater use of short-term advisors and local consultants, a voluntary transfer of managerial authority over resources to local parties allowing these to organise themselves for personnel, capacity development and training and embedding programmes in local structures and under local control.

In the late nineties this debate about the relevance, efficiency, effectiveness and sustainability of personnel services, Technical Cooperation and CD support continued.[19] Major outcomes of these discussions include that CD should be demand driven; organisations should define their own CD objectives as well as themselves identify parties that provide CD support. Furthermore, organisations should define their own measurable objectives and indicators. In theory this is a correct 'party line'. It does, however, require a certain degree of organisational awareness; or more accurately a level of understanding for both the organisation and its leaders regarding current competencies, capabilities and capacity. Organisations should 'know what they do not know' and what competencies and collective capability they possess to formulate a CD process and how best to negotiate with CD suppliers. Where organisational capacities are relative weak, such a situation is, however, often lacking.

Organisations that have a long standing relationship with each other that is based on mutual trust, respect and reciprocity quite often have value adding abilities in such situations. This is because CD support can now be identified and provided without compromising on issues of ownership. 'Quality of the partnership may, therefore, be identified as an important determining factor for effective support to Capacity Development'.[20]

Capacity development is not a mystery: 'what is holding us captive'

For many years Peter Morgan's quote '. . . capacity building is a risky, murky, messy business, with unpredictable and unquantifiable outcomes, uncertain methodologies, contested objectives, many unintended consequences, little credit to its champions and long-time lags'[21] has been the leading line of thought in the debate surrounding capacity development. Some even speak of 'the mystery of capacity development'.[22] In the mean time, however, a very substantial body of knowledge has emerged about capacity, capacity development and capacity development support especially at policy and strategic level.[23] Conceptual coherence and consensus seems to be growing.

Due to these trends, it is high time that the mystery of CD is demystified. Preferred practices are well known, so it is now more a matter of applying the lessons that have been learned over the past decade. The gap between rhetoric and practice is far too big. More attention needs to be paid to the question; 'what is holding us captive?' Such an investigation may lead to exploration of power relations in the international aid system that have profound influence on capacity development and a two-way process of learning and change that is often missing.[24]

Content of the various chapters

The *first* chapter, *Capacity Development; A Brief Overview of the Present State of Affairs* may be considered as a primer, an introduction into the subject of capacity development. Attention is paid to the 'why' of capacity development; different schools of thought in terms of the 'images of organisations'; 'what' is capacity development; characteristics of a capacity development process; types of change; role of outsiders and funding agencies; basic principles. The chapter has emerged from trainings provided by Context, international cooperation for the Centre for International Development Issues Nijmegen, Radboud University Nijmegen, the Netherlands Institute for Southern Africa and staff members of the funding agency Hivos.

The *second* chapter, *Organisational Development and Institutional Development: Case Study Cecoedecon India* is a collective effort by a group of staff members of the Non-Governmental Development Organisation Cecoedecon, one of the biggest and most prestigious development organisations in North India, especially in Rajasthan State. The authors provide an in-depth and authentic account of the organisational change process that was carried out in Cecoedecon. They provide a view 'from below and from within' and pay not only attention to official, visible and politically correct experiences of such a change process, but share feelings, fears and joy as well. This makes their story quite a unique contribution to the existing literature surrounding change processes.

In the *third* chapter, *Learning in Development Organisations: Some Reflections about the Relationship between the Dutch Government and Civil Society Organisations in the Netherlands*, which has been co-authored by Sarah Cummings, focus is placed on learning in the context of the relationship between the Dutch Government and civil society organisations in the Netherlands. The main messages of the chapter are that 'failure to learn from failure' is most probably one of the greatest shortcomings of the development sector; policies, instruments and procedures within the development sector are quite often based on contemporary versions of the modernisation theory and too often based on the assumption that development can be seen as a rather linear process instead of acknowledging that development and change are complex and chaotic processes; that stakeholders may have different perceptions of the same situation or 'reality'; that knowledge benefits most often accrue to the donor or development organisation rather than to the Southern partners. Moreover in this chapter attention is paid to characteristics of a learning organisation.

In the last, *fourth* chapter, *Ten dilemmas concerning capacity development* which has contributions by Udan Fernando, ten major dilemmas with regard to capacity development are listed. The main argument of the chapter is that CD is a multi-facetted process, which has many tacit dimensions and 'hidden connections', that multi-actors are involved (not only 'them' but 'us' as well) and that CD concerns first and foremost people: individuals are key. In conclusion it is argued that 'the mystery of CD needs to be demystified'. Over the last decade considerable progress has been made in defining CD. A whole body of literature has emerged that provides rather deep insights into the ins and outs of CD. It is, therefore, concluded that the emphasis should no longer be on distilling good practices with regard to CD, but on applying the lessons that have been learnt, as the gap between rhetoric and reality is often too big.

Acknowledgements

As indicated in the previous paragraph this book is the product of intensive dialogue and cooperation with a number of individuals and organisations from different parts of the globe. In a way it is a product of co-creation.

I acknowledge, and I am grateful, for opportunities offered and directly or indirectly encouragement and support which I received from: Naa-Aku Acquaye-Baddoo, Karin Baumans, Jessie Bokhoven, Harry Boyte, Edgar Brueser, Karel Chambille, Hope Chigudu, Sarah Cummings, Marleen Deuss, Pradeep Esteves, Sathyasree Goswami, Rafaela Feddes, Udan Fernando, Alan Fowler, Marleen Hasselerharm, Paul Hoebink, Peter Huisman, Bangani Ngeleza, Sharad Joshi, Allan Kaplan, Martin Kariongi Ole Sanago, Piet de Lange, Anne-Marie Leenknegt, (late) Wim van Leeuwen, Lynette Maart, Chiku Malunga, Tom Olila, Neema Pant, P.M. Paul, Malla Reddy, Elise Reynolds, Jyotsna Roy, Anne-Marie Schreven, Lau Schulpen, Titus van der Spek, James Taylor, Lebesech Tsega, Jan Ubels, Fantahun Wakie, Hettie Walters, Bob van der Winden and Sjoerd Zanen.

In addition I wish to thank all those within the organisations with whom we have been working together over the last few years about the subject of capacity development and my current colleagues at Context, international cooperation: Kinsi Amin Eillyas, Pol De Greve, Marloes van Hooijdonk, Tamar van der Leeuw, Hotze Lont, Petra van Os, Menno Salverda, Titus van der Spek and Marieke Sterenborg.

It speaks for itself that, despite this often intensive collaboration I am responsible for all weaknesses, mistakes and shortcomings of this publication.

REFERENCES

1. Pol De Greve, Malla Reddy and Titus van der Spek provided valuable feedback towards the draft version of this Introduction.
2. Ref, e.g., international High Level Forum process on Aid Effectiveness – established as the 'Paris Principles' and its final review in Busan, Korea, 2011.
3. ECDPM, 2008.
4. IOB, 2011; Huyse *et al.*, 2010, Van der Velden & Fernando, 2011, the contribution of James and other IDS staff members in IDS Bulletin (41), 2010; Ubels *et al.*, 2010.
5. Competencies are 'the mind-sets, skills and motivations of individuals which are an essential part of the broader concept of capacity'.

Capabilities (referred to as collective capabilities) are understood as 'the skills of a system or organisation to carry out a particular function or process. It is what enables an organisation to do things and sustain itself'. Capacity, finally, is 'that emergent combination of individual competencies, [collective] capabilities, assets and relationships that enables a human system [or organisation] to create value'. Baser & Morgan, 2008: 3.

6. For a brief history of Technical Assistance reference is made to Hoebink & Van der Velden (2002); Van der Velden & Zweers (1997).
7. UNDP, 2009.
8. Peter Drucker in various publications.
9. Taylor, 2009: 16.
10. In the terminology of Capra (2002) 'hidden connections' (the tacit dimensions of change processes) and capacity development support providers have to become 'artist of the invisible' (Kaplan, 2002).
11. Wigboldus *et al.*, 2011: vii.
12. Nussbaum, 2011: 35. (Italics in the original.)
13. *Ibid.*
14. Recent action research indicates that it is important to have a theory of change in place about among others the interrelatedness between change at the individual level (Human Resources Development), organisational level (Organisational Development) and institutional level (Institutional Development). Ref. Phlix *et al.*, 2012.
15. Ref. Van der Velden & Fernando, 2011: 76, 85, 89.
16. Hivos, 2009:1.
17. Van der Velden & Fernando, 2011: 89.
18. Berg, 1993.
19. Berg, 1993; Fukuda-Parr, Lopes & Malik (eds.), 2002; Browne, (ed.), 2002; Lopes, & Theisohn, 2003.
20. Huyse, 2010: 95.
21. Morgan, 1998: 16.
22. Ref., e.g., Gosses, 2007.
23. Among the more recent publications are: Baser & Morgan, 2008; Ubels *et al.*, 2010; IOB, 2011.
24. James, 2010: 15.

Chapter I

Capacity Development: A Brief Overview of the Present State of Affairs

Fons van der Velden

Introduction: from expressions of solidarity to results

During the last two decades, 'capacity development' has become an important catch phrase in the development sector. This is related to a number of interrelated factors which may be summarised as follows.

The current technocratic approach to development, which is embodied among others in the Millennium Development Goals (MDGs), is under siege. The MDGs are essentially an example of providing services and financial means to the poor and trying to push reforms at State level. This top-down approach ignores many insights that have emerged over the past decades, including the insight that development is basically — implicitly or explicitly — a political process with human beings at the centre and that it is a matter of changing power relations.[1] The theories of Amartya Sen, and the many publications that are built around them, approach poverty in terms of lack of access, and have strengthened the multidimensional approach to poverty analysis. They also stress the importance of focusing on capacities and capabilities.[2] The aim of human development is to create freedom and opportunities for people to develop themselves. Creating these conditions requires a political programme and further development of capacities and capabilities.[3]

Then there is the Aid Effectiveness debate which has given additional momentum to the issue of capacity development. The Paris Declaration (2005) poses very pertinent questions about aid effectiveness around problematic issues such as 'projectitis', failure of structural adjustment, lack of coordination, overburdening local administration and lack of ownership. The Accra Agenda (2008), which does not only focus on 'aid' but on 'development' in general, confirms that developing countries and development organisations need robust capacity to fully own and manage their development processes and to achieve their economic, social and environmental goals. The Accra resolution reads: 'Without robust capacity — strong institutions, systems, and local expertise — developing countries cannot fully own and manage their development processes. We agreed in the Paris Declaration that capacity development is the responsibility of developing countries, with donors playing a supportive role, and that technical cooperation is one of the means to develop capacity. Together, developing countries and donors will take the following actions to strengthen capacity development:

(a) Developing countries will systematically identify areas where there is a need to strengthen the capacity to perform and deliver services at all levels — national, sub-national, sectoral, and thematic — and design strategies to address them. Donors will strengthen their own capacity and skills to be more responsive to developing countries' needs.
(b) Donors' support for capacity development will be demand-driven and designed to support country ownership.
(c) Developing countries and donors will work together at all levels to promote operational changes that make capacity development support more effective.

A third important development that has contributed to the attention paid to capacity development is the realisation that change and development processes are not linear processes that move in a single predictable direction; they are too complex to be summarised in a Log Framework Approach (LFA) model and they do not run the same course everywhere. Often conditions are complicated, complex, or chaotic and differ from place to place (see the diagram below).[4] Patton speaks about six characteristics of complex systems: nonlinear, emergence, adaptive, uncertainty, dynamical and coevolutionary.[5]

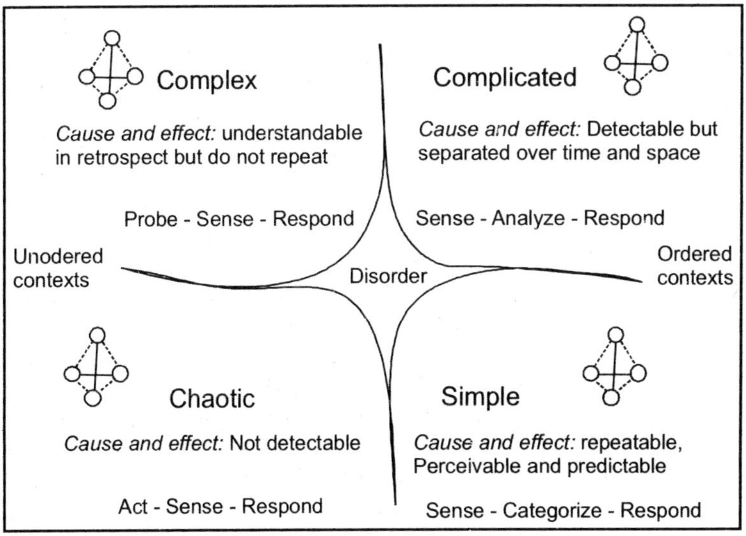

Diagram 1.1: The Cynefin framework

Moreover, the pace of change can vary significantly. These realisations require that development actors have the ability 'to think on their feet'[6], and adjust their approaches, strategies and programmes as per the emerging situations. This requires adequate human resources as well as organisational and institutional capacities.

In assessing the capacity of development actors and development projects and programmes, five different dimensions may in principle be distinguished:

(a) *Context*: Relevance and appropriateness and the

strategic positioning of an organisation or programme ('Positioning').

(b) *Organisational Issues*: The degree of synergy and compatibility of the shared values (mission, vision), strategy, organisational set-up, systems, procedures, et cetera of the development actor ('being').

(c) *Programme Performance*: Effectiveness and efficiency of the programmes which are being carried out by the organisation ('doing').

(d) *Linkages*: Relationships with primary, secondary and tertiary stakeholders ('relating').

(e) *Learnings:* Overall learnings and reflections about the future ('adapting').[7]

From the mid-1980s onwards the above developments have led to a shift in orientation in the development sector from assessment of 'intentions' (emphasis on assessment/analysis of aims and objectives and planned activities) towards organisational capacities. Table 1.1 captures the various stages of the different approaches that are being practiced for programme appraisal.

It may vary from organisation to organisation but in general terms many bilateral, multilateral and private (funding) agencies find themselves in the transition from the 'Result Based Management' era towards a stronger focus on learning. As will be elaborated in the next chapter, such a development is also emerging within capacity enhancement, where in recent years attention for both Monitoring and Evaluation and organisational learning have emerged as important priorities during the organisational change process.

Different views on organisations

Capacity development is an ongoing subject of debate within the development sector. This debate is not only informed by the contextual and political dimensions (see above), but also

Table 1.1: Overview of project and programme appraisal foci in development sector

No.	Main emphasis in terms of appraisal	Characteristics
1.	Initial stage: Establishing relationships	- Starting or enhancing relationships between agencies from North and South. - Emphasis on expressing 'solidarity'.
2.	'Intentions'	- Emphasis on assessment/analysis of aims and objectives and planned activities.
3.	Results (Result Based Management)	- Emphasis on results in terms of output and outcomes. - Increased attention for Planning, Monitoring and Evaluation approaches, systems and tools. - Emphasis on accountability and control. - Emergence of LFA and related tools.
4.	Capacity assessment	- Emphasis on the capacities of individuals and within organisations and institutions. - Emergence of various capacity assessment models from organisations such as INTRAC, I/C Consult, IRDC, ECDPM etc.
5.	Learning	- Emphasis on institutional capacities. - Shift from emphasis on accountability to (organisational) learning. - Capacity development is more and more understood as a collective process of learning in action for social change.[8] - Emphasis on learning capacities and capabilities - Trust based relationships
6.	Adaptive management	- Accepting and implementing implications of learning at management level

by the various views of organisations as held by the participants in the discussion.

In the context of capacity development it is important to assess the capacity of organisations adequately. This point is also emphasised by Gareth Morgan: 'Effective managers and professionals . . . . . have to become skilled in the art of 'reading' the situations they are attempting to change, organise or manage . . . . . They should have a capacity to remain open and flexible, suspending immediate judgements whenever possible, until a more comprehensive view of the situation emerges'.[9]

Generally an organisation is defined as 'A group of people who is willing to accomplish certain goals and for that purpose has agreed on a suitable arrangement'. In management and organisational literature several models have been developed to describe and analyse ('read') organisations.[10] The 7S-model of McKinsey provides a comprehensive overview of organisational aspects.

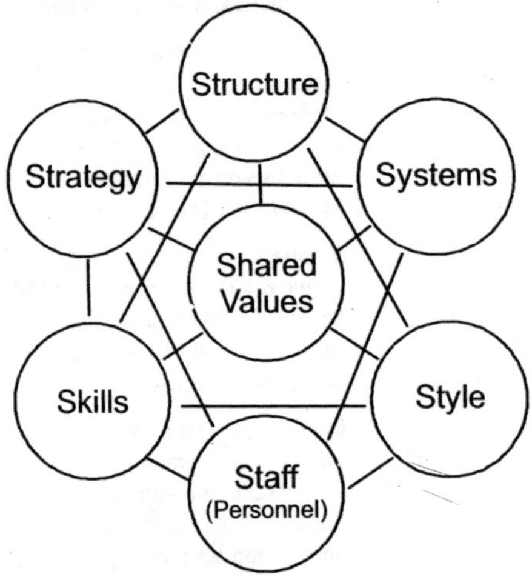

Diagram 1.2: The 7S-model of McKinsey

The 7S McKinsey model is based on 7 S-words: *Shared values*, also called superordinate goals, have to do with guiding concepts, values and aspirations that unite an organisation in some common purpose. They are often reflected in a mission statement, but can also be phrased in a simple slogan. *Strategy*: It should be taken into account that the execution of strategies usually causes bigger problems than their development. *Structure*: For successful organisations it is important to hold on to basic structural divisions, although the structure may be temporarily changed in order to cope with specific strategic tasks. *Systems* consist of all informal or formal procedures that allow the organisation to function, including capital budgeting, training and accounting systems. *Style* refers to the pattern of substantive and symbolic actions undertaken by top managers while *Staff* should be regarded as valuable resources. *Skills* refer to those activities an organisation does best and for which it is known.[11]

Over the last few years, a number of individuals and institutions have contributed to the adaptation of the 7S-model and similar models from the corporate sector to the development sector. The first step is the recognition that these various organisational components should not be studied in isolation but within the broader context, programmes and linkages of development organisations. Thereby the contents of the various aspects and the inter-relatedness and the relationship between the various components are of crucial importance. INTRAC has translated this into 'being' (organisational issues), 'doing' (programmes) and 'relating' (linkages).[12] The relationship can be symbolised as shown in Diagram 1.3.

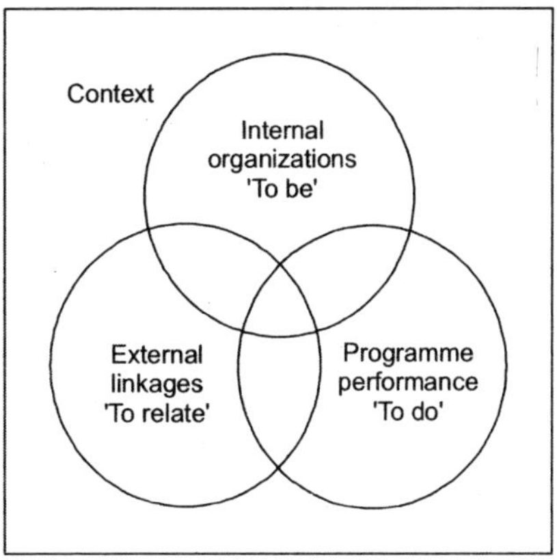

Diagram 1.3: Position of organisation in its context: 'being', 'doing', 'relating'

I/C Consult distinguishes a fourth organisational process: learning.[13]

There is a certain hierarchy or logical order in the various components of an organisational structure. These can be symbolised by the pyramid, as in the Diagram 1.4.

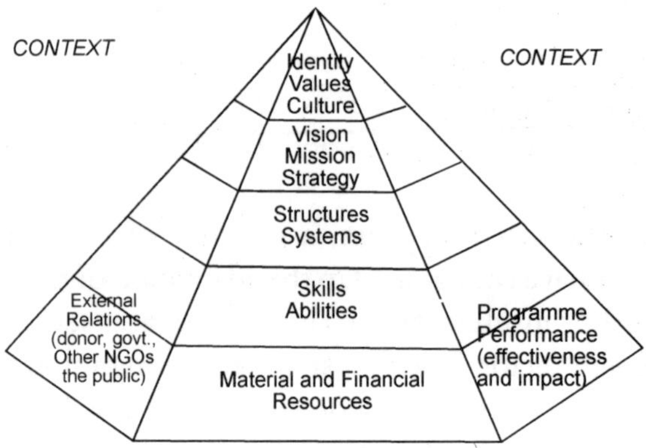

Diagram 1.4: Levels of organisational complexity

The 'shared values', the soul of an organisation[14], shapes all the other components. This echoes the old adage that 'form follows function'. But, as has been indicated by Fowler and others, the process of organisational development will show a spiral rather than a linear line.[15]

It should furthermore be noted that both a balance and imbalance between the various aspects is required: balance enhances efficiency and effectiveness; imbalance facilitates change. A healthy tension between the various components is therefore, required.

The organisational (assessment) models listed here have one major limitation in common: insufficient attention is being paid to tacit aspects of organisations. It is not sufficiently acknowledged that organisations are living entities.

The various models contain to a certain degree a rather mechanistic vision of organisations. In terms of metaphors, organisations are seen in the traditional Frederick Taylor kind of manner as a 'machine' instead of a 'living organism'.[16] Within such an approach the emphasis is on formal structures, systems and procedures, et cetera, and organisational capacity is something that can be engineered from outside an organisation as per Taylor's principles of 'scientific management'.[17] 'Such a logic is premised on a notion of people, organisations and systems as pieces of performance machinery whose capacity

Box 1.1: Images of organisations[18]

According to Gareth Morgan 'all theories of organisation and management are based on implicit images or metaphors that lead us to see, understand, and manage organisations in distinctive yet partial ways'. He has come up with eight images of organisations which are being used by managers and Organisational and Institutional Development (OD/ID) practitioners. These images are:

- *Machines*: In this mechanical way of viewing, which is very much ingrained in everyday conceptions of organisations, organisations are made up of interlocking parts that each play a clearly defined role in the functioning of the whole.
- *Organisms*: This metaphor focuses attention on understanding and managing organisational 'needs' and environmental relations, considering different types of organisations as belonging to different species suitable for different environments.
- *Brains*: This metaphor draws attention to the importance of information processing, learning and intelligence, and provides principles for 'learning organisations'.
- *Cultures*: The main spotlight of this metaphor is on the values, ideas, beliefs, norms, rituals and other patterns of shared meaning that guide organisational life.
- *Political Systems*: This metaphor is used to focus on the different sets of interests, conflicts, and power plays that shape organisational activities ('the politics of organisational life').
- *Psychic Prisons*: This more abstract metaphor examines organisational life to see if, and in what ways, we have become trapped by conscious and unconscious processes of our own creation.
- *Flux and Transformation*: The focus of this metaphor is on the logics of organisational change and on how this change can be understood and managed.
- *Instruments of Domination*: Here the emphasis is the potentially exploitative aspects of organisations; this image can be useful for understanding organisations from the perspective of exploited groups.

Each of these images can create powerful insights, but no single image will provide a perfect or all-purpose point of view. Therefore Morgan emphasises that 'the challenge is to become skilled in the art of using metaphors and images' in order to generate a range of complementary and competing insights.

can be constructed and adjusted through a set of purposeful (and often externally financed and managed) interventions. This logic tends to underestimate the importance of politics, culture and historical contexts, and to rely on the application of 'best practice' solutions across contexts.[19]

When organisations are seen as 'living organisms' the emphasis shifts to tacit aspects and openness to the outside world, allowing for chaos and tension and a strong sense of community and collective identity around a set of common values and common learning. One speaks in this context of 'communities of practice', which are characterised by mutual engagement of its members, a joint activity and, over time, a shared repertoire of routines, tacit rules of conduct and knowledge. Capra calls this the 'dynamics of culture'.[20]

Hofstede and Schein use the onion metaphor to analyse organisations, presenting culture as the personality of an organisation. They emphasise the importance of assessing the deeper, worldview, cultural aspects of an organisation by paying attention to different layers of the organisation. It is important to go to the heart of the matter by 'unpeeling' these layers.

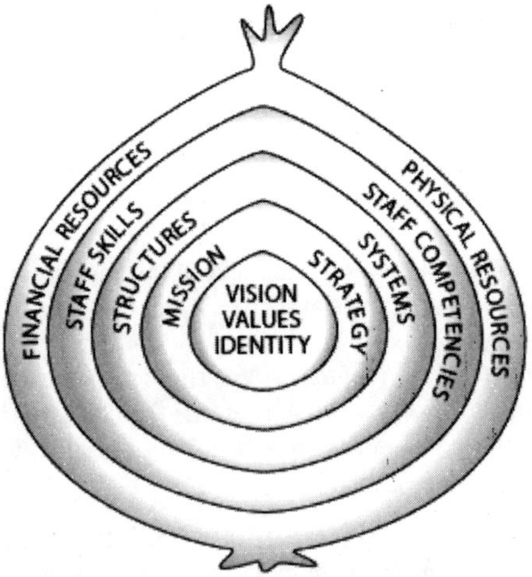

Diagram 1.5: Onion metaphor to analyse organisations

Now-a-days it is common knowledge among management theorists and Organisational Development practitioners that if organisations are perceived and managed in strictly mechanistic ways, they cannot survive in today's complex, knowledge-intensive and rapidly changing environment.[21] Furthermore, if organisations are analysed along those lines, only a limited view of the complex reality will emerge. When organisations are seen as living entities, the continuous interplay of its informal dimensions and its formal manifestations are being acknowledged and reckoned with. Learning and adaptation comes from within, knowledge is embodied in the people within the system and the aliveness of the organisation resides in its informal communities of practice. The emphasis is more on tacit than explicit knowledge ('on what is below the tip of the iceberg').[22]

Not only is it realised more and more that organisations are living entities but also that organisations are open systems with permeable boundaries, in which many co-creators participate to convert inputs into outputs, outcomes and sustainable results.

A more recent model for capacity assessment has been introduced by ECDPM (the European Centre for Development Policy Management[23]) (see further on for more information).[24] The 5C model views organisations as open systems and this has been taken as a starting point, as illustrated in the Diagram 1.6.

In order to make the process of organisational assessment and change within organisations meaningful, various stakeholders need to be involved right from the start. It is necessary to get their active participation and to provide an environment in which their creativity can flourish.[25]

Defining capacity development

A certain conceptual 'muddiness', as Brenda Lipson calls it, exists concerning the meaning of capacity development.[26] It is, therefore, important to define the major conceptual components in more detail.

The UNDP defines capacity as 'the ability of individuals, institutions and societies to perform functions, solve problems

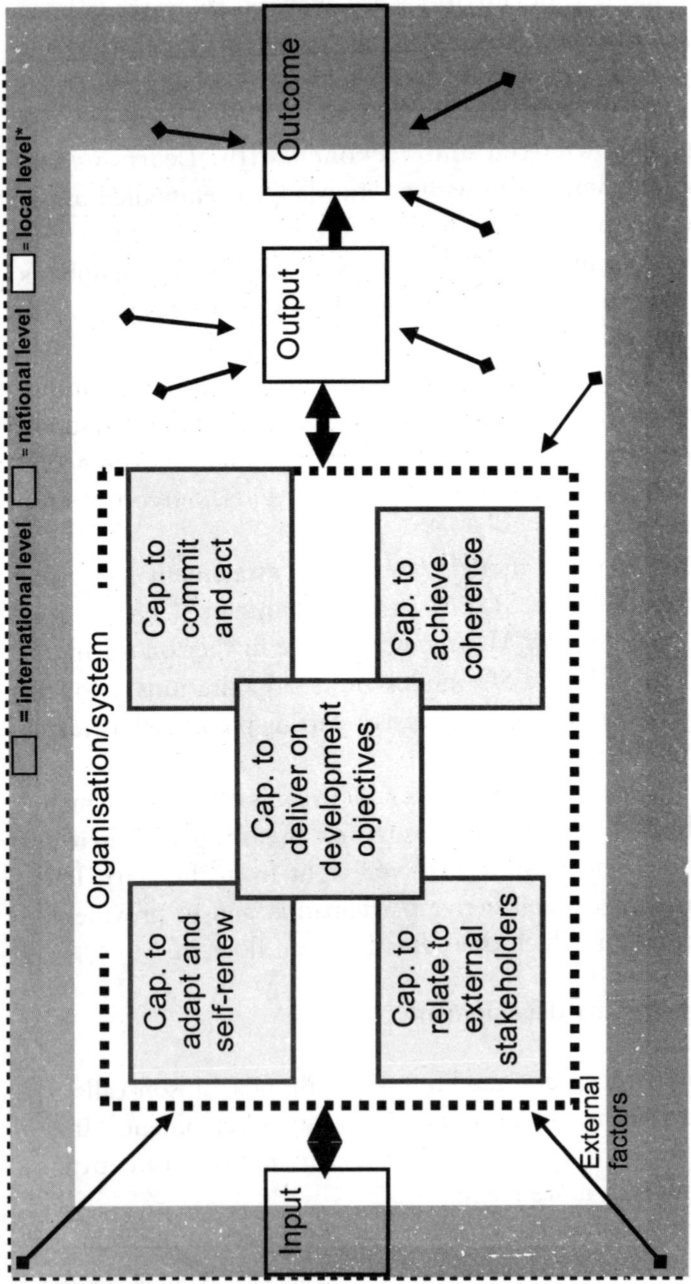

Diagram 1.6: 5C Model of ECDPM

and set and achieve objectives in a sustainable manner'.[27] The Development Assistance Committee of the OECD applies the following definition: 'The ability of people, organisations and society as a whole to manage their affairs successfully'.[28]

Capacity development is defined by UNDP as 'the process through which individuals, organisations and societies obtain, strengthen and maintain the capabilities to set and achieve their own objectives over time'. OECD DAC perceives capacity development as 'the process whereby people, organisations and societies as a whole unleash, strengthen, create, adapt and maintain capacity over time'.[29] Both definitions indicate the process rather than technical support but speak about maintaining capabilities or capacity. There is, however, a slight difference in emphasis; the UNDP definitions (still) reflect the ambition of a process that can be controlled and clearly measured while OECD sees capacity development more as a process, and is more able 'to let go'.

These definitions reflect instrumental or functional approaches to capacity and capacity development with a heavy emphasis on performance related notions of capacity (the ability 'to do').

However, describing capacity only as performance-related is insufficient — it is also concerned with the ability or 'power within', i.e. 'to be' or 'to exist'. This is called intrinsic or robust capacity. Lipson and Hunt describe capacity, therefore, as, 'The opportunity for an individual, group or organisation to use their capabilities in practice'.[30] Allan Kaplan — the erstwhile director of CDRA, Cape Town, South Africa — defines capacity as ' ... the ability of an organisation to function as a resilient, strategic and autonomous entity ..... [which is] capable of sovereign focus and direction, to changing circumstances, and of acting decisively to impact on, and change'.[31] In other words capacity is linked to the ability to achieve the mission of an organisation and perform official and unofficial, visible and invisible organisational functions.

Clarke and Oswald have identified three different

perspectives in relation to the origin and value of the term capacity development, which should not be understood as mutually exclusive alternatives.[32] These three perspectives can be summarised as follows:

1. A technical solution to a technical problem.
2. A discourse concealing an agenda for power.
3. An aspiration for emancipatory development.

The first is the predominant perspective in the literature, and concentrates on the issue of aid and development effectiveness (*ref.* Paris Agenda, Accra Declaration, et cetera). Secondly, others, such as Kühl, see capacity development as 'a political technology of neoliberal governance'.[33] The third school of thought uses the term as an aspiration for social justice. From this perspective, capacity development is an end in itself closely related to emancipatory development. Within this context, Clark & Oswald argue that capacity development should be understood as 'a collective process of learning in action for social change. Support for capacity development processes demands a critical development practice that implies mutual learning, with an emphasis on reflective and experiential approaches'.[34]

In line with Kaplan's definition, capacity development can be defined as '. . . . . the increased ability and power to do something in particular (functional capacity), or increase resilience and autonomy (intrinsic capacity)'.[35] This definition conveys the notion of change process well — there is no conscious intervention about capacity development; no 'agency' whether internal or external.[36] Capacity building refers to support to capacity development, to capacity enhancement. 'It is a purposeful, conscious effort to bring about capacity development'.[37] In this context it is important to note that 'building' does not imply starting from scratch. 'Capacity building' suggests a purpose to the activities, whereas 'capacity development' may be viewed as a broader term which can cover a process with no involvement of 'agency' i.e., no purposeful intervention.[38]

Capacity relates to competencies — energies, skills and abilities of individuals. Capabilities relate to a collective ability of a group or a system to do something. Tacit aspects of capacity such as experience, intuition and institutional memory are aspects that cannot be documented.

Different levels of capacity and capacity development can be distinguished:

1. Individual;
2. Group, team, department;
3. Organisational;
4. Institutional;
5. Societal;
6. Social capital; and
7. International.

Capacity enhancement relates, therefore, to individuals (Human Resource Development, HRD), organisations [e.g., Organisational Development (OD)] and the broader context [Systems Development (SD)]. The combination of these factors leads to Institutional Development (ID). Table 1.2 presents these levels and the focus of capacity development they imply.

Table 1.2: HRD, OD, SD[39]

Institutional development		
Process dimension	Levels	Focus
Human Resource Development	1. Individuals and groups	Competence, motivation
Organisational Development	2. Organisations	Structures, processes and systems
System Development	3. Network linkages	• Patterns of communication/ collaboration between organisations
	4. Sector	• Policies, rules, legislative framework
	5. Overall context	• Macro-level policies and conditions
		• Cultural values, norms and traditions

In the literature on this subject capacities are often divided into hard and soft. Soft capacities have been divided into tangible and intangible.[40] The former consist of the visible systems and processes that may be in place; the latter refer to less visible capacities such as the capacity to establish relationships. Whilst hard and soft, as well as tangible and intangible capacities are all important, it is the soft and intangible capacities that are difficult to identify and 'develop'.[41] Baser and Morgan support this view in the ECDPM study on capacity, which found that in many cases, intangibles such as identity and confidence were of major significance in processes of capacity development.

In various models different elements of capacity are distinguished. In the five capabilities model (5C model), which was developed by Baser and Morgan[42], five interrelated core capabilities are identified which provide a basis for the assessment of a particular situation at any given moment.

The five elements of capacity distinguished by Baser and Morgan are:

1. Capability to deliver on development objectives.
2. Capability to act and commit.
3. Capability to adapt and self-renew.
4. Capability to relate to external stakeholders.
5. Capability to achieve coherence.

The essence of the five core capabilities is presented in the Diagram 1.7.

Character of capacity development

As indicated in the foregoing, capacity development and building is not an aim in itself. Such processes are aimed/undertaken to improve the resilience, bargaining capacity (power) and/or efficiency, effectiveness (project or programme implementation) capacity of an organisation. Capacity development and building are linked to organisational performance.

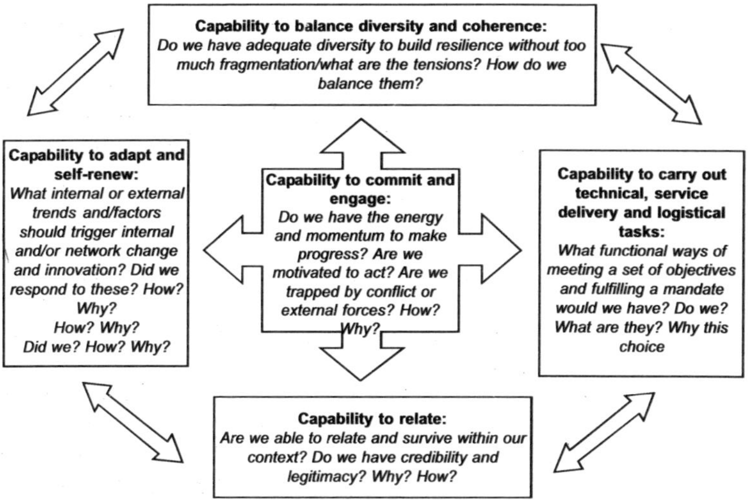

Diagram 1.7: 5C Model (Baser & Morgan)

Due to the organic and open nature of organisations as systems and the complex and sometimes ambiguous nature of capacity development and building processes, it is not always appropriate to think that a planned, linear design will ensure predetermined outcomes. Peter Morgan has summarised the character of such processes succinctly: 'It is a risky, murky and messy business, with unpredictable outcomes'.[43]

Peter Senge has introduced the principle of healthy tension which basically indicated the gap, the difference between aspired organisational functioning and actual functioning (see Diagram 1.8).

If there is no tension, an organisation will become stagnant; if the tension between aspired and actual position is too big it will be difficult to bridge the gap.

In view of the above the emphasis or focus of capacity development can target different areas or different organisational characteristics. When the focus is on the position of an organisation in view of the context, and its strategic positioning *vis-à-vis* other stakeholders, the emphasis is normally on Institutional Development. The focus can furthermore be on organisational dimensions, soft or hard;

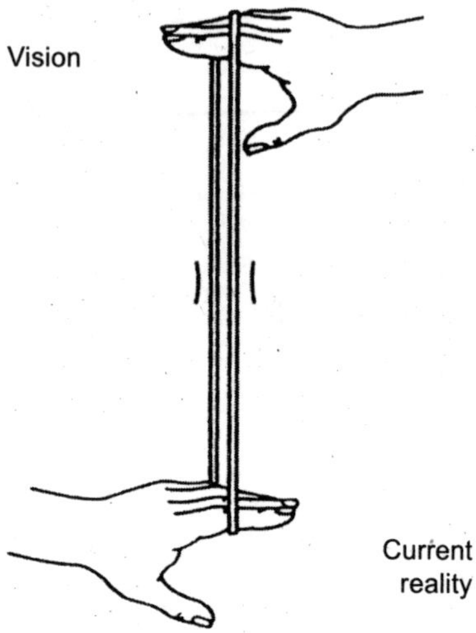

Diagram 1.8: The principle of healthy tension

visible or invisible; or one of the seven components mentioned by McKinsey.

During the last few years more and more capacity development professionals have realised that capacity development is at a crossroads; many practitioners are experiencing uncertainties in defining their purposes, practice and relationships. Awareness is emerging that leading or facilitating transformation of organisations and/or institutions calls for a deeper understanding of change and a new set of approaches, strategies, and skills. Some argue that this means that those who are facilitating change 'must transform in order to lead transformation successfully'.[44]

Contrary to the traditional organisational and institutional development approaches, many OD practitioners now-a-days realise that a conscious transformation of organisations and institutions requires a multi-dimensional approach to transformation. Such a strategy requires that competent attention be paid to three inter-related critical components of a change strategy: (1) content; (2) people; and (3) process (see Diagram 1.9).

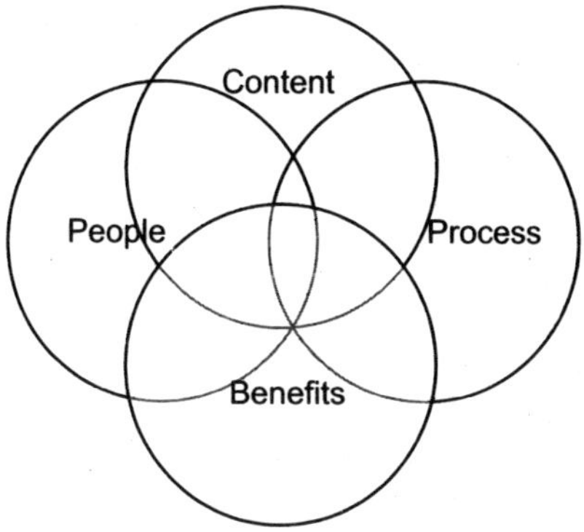

Diagram 1.9: Multidimensional approach of facilitating organisational change[45]

'Content' refers to 'what' about the organisation needs to change. About what is happening in the external domain, a specific 'market' in terms of dynamics with regard to hard and soft ware and how this is reflected within organisations and institutions in terms of issues such as strategy, structure, systems, process, technology, work practices et cetera.

'People' refers to behaviours, emotions, minds and spirits of the human beings who are designing, implementing, supporting, or being impacted by the change (mostly internal domains).

'Process' refers to *how* 'content' and 'people' changes need to be planned, designed and implemented. There are many different definitions and meanings of the term process, but in the present context process may be defined as 'The natural or intentional unfolding of continuous events towards a desired outcome'.[46] Process denotes the actions that produce both the external (content) and internal (people) changes. Process is, as Schein puts it succinctly, 'how things are done between people and in groups'.[47]

In recent studies it has been argued that all these three areas must be integrated in one unified transformational effort that moves an organisation from where it is today to where it chooses to be in the future. Anderson and Ackerman Anderson argue that '. . . . . organisations that take a piecemeal approach and separate their organisational and technical changes (content) from their human and cultural changes (people) fail dramatically'. They state that a conscious design of a transformation process is a key factor for success and that process, ultimately, determines the success of the change implementation.[48]

Within the context of the above it is important to define what type of change is being pursued. In the current management literature quite a number of different forms of change are distinguished.[49] Anderson & Ackerman Anderson have summarised the literature about this subject in the following three archetypes of organisational change.

Developmental Change basically represents the improvement of an existing situation and in metaphorical terms is normally 'within the box' of what is already known or practised. The key focus is to strengthen or correct what already exists in an organisation, thus ensuring improved performance, continuity and greater satisfaction.

Transitional Change is more complex. It is the required response to more significant shifts in environmental forces or marketplace requirements for success. Rather than simply improve 'what is', transitional change replaces 'what is' with something entirely different. The organisation must dismantle and let go of the old way of operating and move through a transition while the new state is being put into practice.

In *Transformational Change*, human and cultural issues are normally the key drivers. Transformational Change is, simply said, the radical shift from one state of being to another, so significant that it requires a shift of culture, behaviour and mind set to be implemented successfully and sustained over time. '. . . . . in other words, transformation demands a shift in human awareness that completely alters the way the organisation and its people see the world, their customers, their work and themselves.'[50]

The notions of transitional and transformational change are more in line with the conceptual notions and approaches of the new science worldview of authors such as Capra and Wheatley and OD practitioners such as Kaplan. These notions replace what 'is' with something entirely different.

In sum, developmental change is basically improving current operations, while transitional change is replacing current operations with new ones. Transformational, change however, requires the discovery of a new state which must replace current operations. The first-two change processes are characterised by a process with some degree of control and order, while transformational change is normally a much more chaotic affair, which cannot be controlled and planned so easily.[51] The journey of transformation is anything but a straight and linear line.

Within this context it should be mentioned that none of the types of change is in principle more valuable, feasible or viable than the other, but that each approach serves a different purpose and has a different logic in terms of approaches, methods and tools.

In general terms, the different types of change (developmental, transitional and transformational) are linked to different levels of learning: single, double and deutero learning.[53]

The management of transformational change is, however, a rather unpredictable process that requires giving up any expectation of controlling the process; active pursuit of information and feedback during the process; and optimising the ability to learn from feedback. The last requirement is the crucial one. A learning approach to organisational change is, therefore, an appropriate strategy to implement this type of change. Within such a learning approach it is not only necessary to pay attention to formal organisational characteristics, but also to fundamental assumptions, values, feelings, and to gain deeper clarity about occurring realities.[54]

Box 1.2: Different types of change[52]

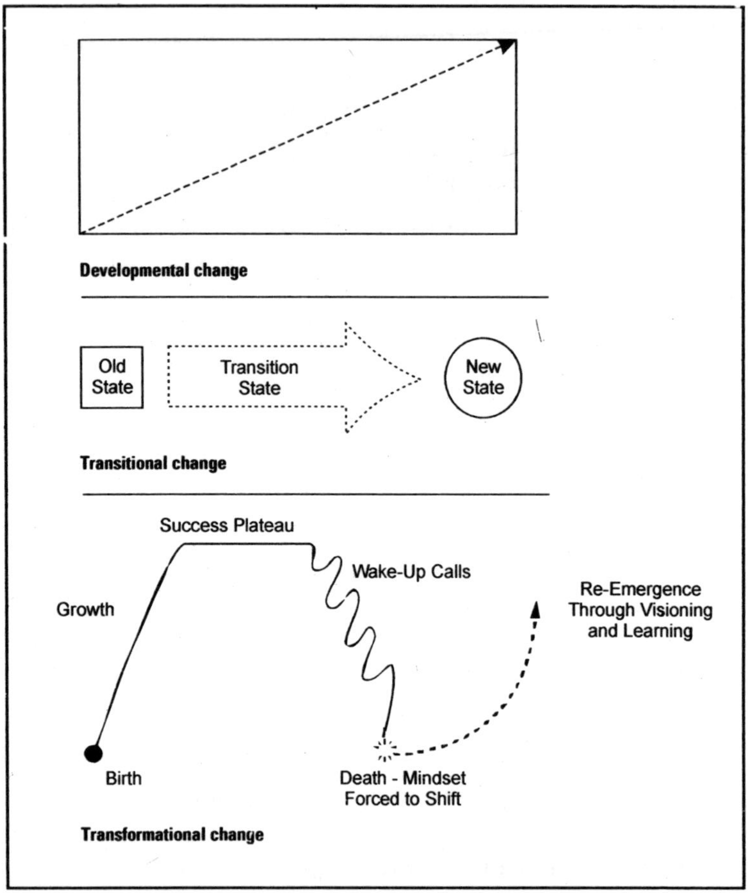

Such a multi-dimensional approach requires that those facilitating change pay attention to the before-mentioned four critical areas: (1) content in terms of the market in which the organisation or the institution is operating; (2) people (mindsets of people involved); (3) process dynamics; (4) results. The realisation of this integrated approach has led to the fact that many no longer speak of organisational or institutional development but about change management, process facilitation or facilitation of change processes.

Change management[55]

Over the years many publications (often in the form of manuals) have appeared with change management tools in general and (self-) assessment tools in particular.[56] The Dutch non-profit consultancy organisation IC/Consult distinguishes four different approaches to organisational assessment.[57] The organisation assessment approach focuses on weaknesses or risks that have been identified in a comprehensive organisation assessment, audit or evaluation. Such an assessment consists of a temporary diagnosis of the organisation, often based on models such as McKinsey's 7S model or INTRAC's 'being, doing and relating' model. The results of such an assessment are used to help set the organisation's priorities for change, which can include various components such as restructuring, system development, management coaching, training, exposure visits, action learning and research.

The strategic planning approach is similar in the sense that it starts with summarising internal and external factors, trends and (expected) events that are relevant for the organisation, and analysing strengths and weaknesses (often using the SWOT method). Consequently, future strategies are generated which are evaluated on a number of criteria, and then translated into operational plans. Here, the assumption is that organisational improvements are linked to strategic choices and the approach is more outward-looking.

The architecture approach is more focused on the links between strategic, organisational and operational choices, and assumes that there is a certain hierarchy, or logic, in the order of choices to be made by an organisation. This hierarchy can be seen in the sequence of: vision – mission – long-term objectives – strategies, etc. The first step in an OD process is, therefore, to renew the choices made in these areas in the given order. Gaps between these areas reveal weaknesses that can be addressed through reorganisations, system development, procedural adjustments et cetera.

Finally, in a learning approach, OD is defined as an organisation's 'ability to understand itself and its external role, in order to learn continually from its practice, renew itself and manage change towards achieving objectives effectively'. It is less concerned with a participative and comprehensive analysis of all strengths and weaknesses, but works immediately on improving the quality of thinking and learning. Its aim is to strengthen the organisation's own ability to adapt rather than making a momentary assessment, but this can sometimes lead to an overemphasis on designing learning processes and neglecting available data.

The first-three approaches have a somewhat normative connotation, i.e., the assumption that there exists a 'best way to organise', while with the learning approaches there is less clarity at the beginning of the process regarding the desired outcome, but there is space for this to unfold in the process. Difference between normative and following approaches (I/C Consult).

Linked with the three different types of change, three archetype of change process can be distinguished: project, systems, and conscious process thinking. Project thinking structures organises activities in a rather linear and sequential manner. This is in many organisations the dominant paradigm and also up to a certain degree reflected in the organisational (self-) assessment approach, strategic planning approach, and organisational architecture approach.[58]

Systems thinking is a way of mapping the interconnected relationships between components of any system. This approach has been promoted by Peter Senge in particular, in the *Fifth Discipline* and many later publications. Senge includes the internal state of people (mindsets) and culture while mapping the forces that play within the system that influences an organisation's current reality and possible achievement of its vision. Most probably this approach is the most complete one available as it attends to the wholeness and interconnectedness across space; continuous process through time; and eternal reality.[59] Such an approach is also a significant evolution from linear thinking to seeing interdependencies, to understanding process dynamics over time, to understanding the role and impact of human consciousness.

Anderson & Ackerman Anderson argue that the innovative approach of Senge *et al.* needs to be brought one step further to what they call conscious process thinking. The word conscious denotes 'being aware of all aspects of process, internal and external, across the levels of individuals, relationships, teams, the whole systems, market place and environment . . . .' Conscious process thinking then means 'seeing reality as a multi-dimensional process, parts/whole connected across space, continuously unfolding through time, affecting both internal and external dimensions at all levels of organisations, from individual to environment'.[60]

The role of relative outsiders[61]

There are in principle a number of different roles that outsiders, such as a consultant or advisor, may play in fostering organisational change. The success of processes of change highly depends on advisors playing the appropriate role at the appropriate time. 'This requires an understanding, appreciation and experience of different roles in order to avoid common pitfalls of consultants playing inappropriate and confused roles'.[62]

In the literature about this subject models are used which describe consulting roles along a directive and non-directive continuum. By directive it is meant that the consultant assumes leadership, initiates and directs actively. This is normally the case in the traditional expert model approach. An advisor provides the client with data which he or she may use or not. The consultant is moderately involved and responsible for results but not so much concerned with client learning. A facilitator is not responsible for results but for helping the client with process-type interventions to make decisions.[63] Schein puts it as follows: 'The expert and doctor model fix the problem; the goal of process facilitation is to increase the client system's *capacity for learning* so that it can in the future fix its own problems'.[64] The position of advisor is somewhere in between the two.

Facilitation is a complex, iterative process, which enables things to happen. In a nutshell, facilitation is all about improving performance and helping others to help themselves. At the heart of process facilitation is the need to build relationships. 'Process facilitation is about forming a relationship with a client that allows the latter to perceive, understand and act on the events that occur in his or her environment in order to improve the situation as defined by him or her.' The ultimate function of a facilitator is 'to teach others how to diagnose and constructively intervene, so that clients are better able to continue improving the organisation, sector or situation on their own'.[65] Facilitating OD/ID processes implies facilitating collective and mutual social learning. It means helping to create the conditions in which individuals understand and share the same kind of development objectives, so that they can and will learn to improve their performance and hence attain more of their objectives.[66]

In recent management literature the discussion about this topic is brought one step further. In addition to the directive non-directive continuum one more position may be added: self-organising. In a self-organising change process, change leaders do not use a structured methodology but allow a transformation process to more or less organise itself. 'Self-organising change leaders do not attempt to control or even heavily influence a change process either by establishing a preliminary process design or by facilitating . . . . Self-organising change leaders nurture the conditions for transformation within the organisation, but allow the actual design and facilitation of the process of change to emerge from the organisation.'[67]

Champion, Kiel and McLendon have developed a Consulting Role Grid (CRG) and identified nine (potential) consulting roles, which may be selected on the preferred intervention style of the consultant, organisational situation and needs, characteristics of the client and the client-consultant relationship. These roles will involve different degrees of intervention on the consultant's part.[68]

Box 1.3: The consulting role grid

Counsellor 'You do it; I will be your sounding board'	**Coach** 'You did well; you can add this next time'	**Partner** 'We will do it together and learn from each other'
Facilitator 'You do it; I will attend to the process'	**Teacher** 'Here are some principles you can use to solve problems of this type'	**Modeller** 'I will do it; you watch so you can learn from me'
Reflective observer 'You do it; I will watch and tell you what I see and hear'	**Technical adviser** 'I will answer your questions as you go along'	**Hands-on expert** 'I will do it for you; I will tell you what to do'

It should be noted that there is no best way to support, facilitate, or encourage change within organisations. Both approach and advisory role must be chosen in accordance with the specific situation, including type of change that is being required, type of organisation and relationship between the organisation and the outside party. At the same time it must be noted that generally speaking the facilitative change approach fits best for the majority of transformational efforts as such an approach contributes to the sustainability of the change effort,[69] while the self-organising style may be the future.

Good practices with regard to capacity development

Based on several decades of experience and research in the area of OD and ID, a number of authors identify certain key principles that should be followed if efforts to enhance capacity of developmental actors are to be effective.[70] As such, these principles provide broad guidelines on which to assess the effectiveness of capacity building support services. Some of these principles relate to the products delivered in a capacity enhancement programme. Others relate to the process that one goes through to build capacity in given organisations. Recent publications basically confirm earlier findings with regard to this issue.[71]

The learnings with regard to this subject have been summarised quite succinctly by Rick James:

> '. . . . . there has been progress in defining capacity development and in distilling good practice. A number of recent studies from a diversity of sources and sectors show there are important emerging areas of conceptual congruence and all agree that capacity development:[72]
>
> - is a complex, human process based on values, emotions, and beliefs;
> - is an internal process (endogenous – 'formed from within') that involves the main actor taking responsibility for the process of change;
> - involves shifts in power and identity;
> - involves changes in relationship between elements of open-systems;
> - is uncertain and unpredictable; and,
> - is powerfully influenced by the culture and the changing context.

In consequence, there is also general agreement on the principles of good practice in capacity development. These resonate with principles highlighted by James and Hailey[73] who assert that good capacity development:

- is a human, client-centred approach that:
  1. is people-centred and engages with values;
  2. ensures client responsibility for change; and

3. addresses issues of power and relationship.

- has a locally appropriate and sustainable delivery process that:
  4. involves a variety of techniques;
  5. explicitly adapts to the particular context and culture; and
  6. uses and develops skilled local capacity building providers.
- is well planned and managed which:
  7. pursues a carefully planned and 'situational' strategy;
  8. focuses on implementation of the change process; and
  9. has developmental resourcing.
- systematically assesses and learns from experience.

While the language may vary, the underlying principles are similar.[74] There is an unusual consensus between a wide diversity of stakeholders about what works in capacity development. The issue then is not about knowledge. 'We know what to do in capacity development. The question is whether we put into practice what we know'.[75]

In reality there is a substantial gap between theory and practice: Northern donors continue to set the agenda for capacity building; contents of capacity development often reflects donor priorities; power relations have a profound influence on capacity development and a two way process of learning and change is often missing. Moreover, support of International NGDOs for development of local capacity development providers is often missing and appears to be more instrumental than strategic; in terms of methods, emphasis is still on training and technical assistance[76] and '. . . . . over-reliance on [these] structured, even formulaic, approaches to capacity development suggests that many agencies are avoiding facing up to some of the messy and complex human dimensions of capacity development'.[77]

From research that has been conducted by INTRAC it may furthermore be concluded that many international NGDOs lack a strategic approach to capacity development.[78] The performance with regard to resourcing is mixed as well as the monitoring and evaluation of capacity development experiences.[79]

'What is holding development practitioners captive?'

If there is so much confirmed evidence about good practices with regard to capacity development and the gap between rhetoric and reality is so big, the question arises 'what is holding the development sector captive' with regard to this issue? A few interrelated issues may be mentioned here.

In general terms the current trends in the overall policies and operational guidelines in the aid system are not conducive for implementation of good development practice by development organisations. Many donors have taken a more state-centred approach over the last few years[80] whereby capacity development becomes less important. Secondly, 'the audit orientation of public sector management (measurable targets, visible results, efficiency) has also permeated the aid world, negatively affecting capacity development. Government donor agencies are increasingly driven by measures of efficiency . . . . This acts as major disincentives to implementing good quality development capacity development'.[81] These developments are aggravated by the fact that more and more International NGDOs become more operational moving away from 'partnerships' with autonomous local organisations.

These factors are influenced by the fact that in many regions not too many good capacity development providers are around.

Role of funding agencies

In his book 'Demystifying organisation development: practical capacity-building experiences of African NGOs' Rick James presents a number of implications for Northern NGOs in supporting organisational development, based on extensive research and case studies with practitioners.[82] First and foremost, he recommends that donors should ensure their core activity of funding is building capacity rather than undermining it. For this, they need two fundamental abilities: knowledge and understanding of the forces of OD as well as the ability to differentiate funding responses. If, however, funding NGOs do decide to play an active role in supporting OD consultancy, this has implications if they are concerned about quality that will be discussed below.

First, they should ensure a better conceptual understanding amongst their staff of organisational strengthening. Most people working in Northern NGOs do not have a theoretical background of management and organisational behaviour and all their understanding is based solely on work experience; this needs to be improved upon. In addition, they need to understand the role they play in the partnership and what this means for (the possibilities and limits of) their role in organisational strengthening. Secondly, Northern NGDOs need to develop strategies for OD. Specifically, they should consider ways in which they can develop a Southern supply of OD services, as this poses a critical constraint. Also, as OD requires deep engagement, they should focus their support on strategically selected partners. Third, it is vital for Northern NGOs who are taking a more active role in OD support to ensure some form of field-based organisational structures. Currently their judgements are based on a fairly superficial basis, while in OD more depth of information and quality of relations are a prerequisite.

Fourth, donor NGOs should develop systems for measuring the impact of organisational strength in order to make an inventory of practice and support learning. For the latter, it is crucial that experiences are shared among NGOs. Fifth, involvement in OD processes has important implications for funding cycles and fund-raising strategies, which should become more long-term, as organisational strengthening takes many years. This also means money will be spent on non-project investments, implying less visible direct results. One-off 'log frames' (which are a result of the Logical Framework Approach) are not required to plan organisational strengthening; a process which changes dramatically over time. And most importantly, the Southern NGDO needs to be in control of the process, including identifying and prioritising how the support money should be spent.

A sixth point refers to the need for additional skills and knowledge of the donor staff, who need to understand how organisations behave and develop in order to support this process appropriately. James' seventh recommendation is that NGDOs cooperate with each other in order to be coherent rather than conflicting in their support. Finally, his eighth recommendation is for donor NGDOs to apply OD principles to their own organisations, as some of the key constraints in improving development efforts lie in the Northern donors' procedures and policies. This has seldom been recognised and, although many Northern NGDOs are undergoing a major identity crisis and are searching for their appropriate role, they have generally not been very open to internal change.

The above-mentioned suggestions for good donor practice with regard to OD/ID remain, very unfortunately, still valid. In view of what we know about capacity development and the need for organisations to know their strengths and weaknesses, Rick James has formulated organisational 'sins' and 'virtues' with regard to capacity development.[83]

Box 1.4: Seven Deadly Sins in Capacity Development

Pride: ***Seeing ourselves as better than others***

Pride may be behind the thinking we have encountered among all stakeholders: we know better what others need; we are OK, but they have a problem; we can control how others develop; we do not need help from others; I cannot admit my faults; we do not need to work with others.

Greed: ***The acquisition of wealth or a longing to possess something***

Preoccupation with securing more funding or fees has undermined the practice of many stakeholders, pushed international agencies to take over work that could be done by local CSOs and prioritised accountability to donors over impact on the poor. It may also be about wanting to retain the power in the relationship.

Lust: ***Seeing others as a means to our gratification***

Our pride and greed give way to lust — a lust for control, power, status. We use other stakeholders as means to our ends. Partnerships exist only in name. Different stakeholders are only interested in what others can provide for them. This instrumental, impure love for others leads to a lack of courage and boldness.

Gluttony: ***Thoughtless excess, over-consumption or habitual greed***

We see this in international over-consumption of limited local human resources for capacity building. We also see this in local CSO 4x4 vehicles overwhelming communities. We see this in inflating salary levels and consultant fees...

Envy: ***A desire to have something possessed by another***

Envy may be at the root of our failure to collaborate with other stakeholders in capacity development. Local capacity development providers see others as competition and fail to work together and learn from each other. INGOs pull local CSOs in different directions with 'their' capacity development activities.

Wrath: ***Intolerance, impatience, discrimination or extreme anger***

Wrath undermines capacity building when it leads to impatience. When artificial project deadlines prove unrealistic, this can lead to frustration and even anger.

Sloth: ***Reluctance to work or make an effort and failure to use/develop talents***

Different stakeholders sometimes do not bother to apply their knowledge and are too lazy to prioritise. We do not actively seek to develop and implement our knowledge about capacity development. We often fail to have the determination to see it through.

Box 1.5: Organisational Virtues in Capacity Development

Humility: ***Modest Behaviour, Selflessness, Giving of Respect – Opposes Pride***

We know capacity development is an endogenous process, not something you can do to another NGO. Therefore, international NGOs need to recognise they cannot do it alone; it is a collective effort. To support capacity development well also requires the humility to be open to learning and change your own organisation if it is inhibiting the process.

Compassion: ***Kindness, Contentment, Satisfaction — Opposes Envy***

Compassion is about putting partner needs first; wanting the best for their organisation, not your needs (e.g., for improved reporting). True compassion includes a sense of justice for the poor. It can be salutary for any INGO to (re) assess their actions against their mission. Sometimes they inadvertently find they are taking a competitive stance towards other INGOs for their own benefit, rather than ultimately for the benefit of the community.

Patience: ***Forbearance, Peace, Ability to Forgive — Opposes Wrath***

Capacity development can be difficult and frustrating. It involves changing power and relationships among stakeholders. People do not change as quickly as we would like. In consequence, for INGOs to be effective, they need to be patient. Capacity development does not always work. It can often be a process of trial and error. INGOs need the patience of character to learn from failure.

Determination: ***Diligence, Passion, Courage — Opposes Sloth***

Good INGOs are relentless in implementing good practice. They have disciplined thought and actions, realistic goals, clear strategy, good practice methods, rigorous monitoring and evaluation systems, innovative organisational learning, flexibility, and accessible documenting. They push themselves to do what is right, not expedient. They demonstrate their commitment to capacity development by investing quality resources (finances, staff and management time).

Generosity: ***Sacrifice — Opposes Greed***

To implement good practice capacity building requires a generous attitude. Generous in sharing learning and in looking into what others can receive from their inputs (not putting their own interests first). Being generous means focusing on what is good and life-giving in a situation, not just the obvious problems.

Self-Control: ***Mindfulness of Other, Temperance — Opposes Gluttony***

Implementing good practice capacity building requires international agencies to be mindful of others and their surrounding context. They exercise self-control, not merely poaching the best local NGO staff because they can pay them more. They are careful stewards of their resources, including staff time.

Honesty: ***Openness, Purity — Opposes Lust***

To implement good capacity development programmes requires honesty. Any agency brings an agenda into a programme. It is important to acknowledge this self-interest in order to be able to manage it and control it. Good international agencies are consistent — being as open with their partners about internal information as they demand them to be.

REFERENCES

1. Bieckmann, 2008.
2. See among others Apsan Frediani, 2010.
3. Sen, 1999.
4. A short introduction about this so-called Cynefin framework can be found at: http://www.youtube.com/watch?v=5mqNcs8mp74 last accessed June 10, 2010. Ref as well: Snowden at http://cognitive-edge.com/library/more/video/introduction-to-the-cynefin-framework/ (last accessed on May 1, 2012).
5. Patton, 2011: 150–151.
6. Soal, 2004.
7. This classifications is inspired by the work of INTRAC (www.intrac.org) and the organisational scan of I/C Consult (www.icconsult.nl)
8. Clark & Oswald, 2010: 1.
9. G. Morgan, 1997.
10. See e.g. James, 1998, Chapter 1.
11. Stoner, 1993: 290-292.
12. Lipson & Hunt, 2008: 15.
13. IC/Consult: www.icconsult.org
14. These words are James Taylor's of CDRA Cape Town, see OD Debate, April 1995.
15. Fowler, 2000, see also I/C Consult, *Looking at organisations* (March 2001), www.icconsult.org
16. The metaphor is borrowed from Peter Senge (1990).
17. Braverman, 1974: 85.
18. G. Morgan, 1997.
19. Land *et al.*, 2009.
20. Capra, 2002: 95.
21. Ref. The publications of among others Capra, De Geus, Kaplan, Senge, Wheatley.
22. Pedler & Aspinwall, 1998: 63.
23. www.ecdpm.org
24. Fowler & Ubels (2010) provide a comparison of the CDRA (Kaplan *et al.*) and ECDPM (Baser & Morgan) approaches to capacity assessment and capacity development.
25. Capra, 2002: 99.
26. Personal communication, January 2010 (Hivos Curriculum).
27. UNDP, 2006.
28. DAC, 2006.
29. Lipson personal communication, January 11, 2010.
30. Lipson & Hunt, 2008.
31. Kaplan, 1999 (cited in Lipson & Hunt, 2008: 11).
32. Clark & Oswald, 2010: 3–4.
33. Kühl, 2009: 575.
34. Clark & Oswald, 2010: 3.

35. Lipson & Hunt, 2008: 31. (It relates to Kolb's experiential learning cycle of reflecting; connecting; testing; doing.)
36. Lipson personal communication, January 11, 2010.
37. *Ibid*.
38. Lipson & Hunt, 2008: 31.
39. Kruse, 1998: 17.
40. Kaplan, 1999.
41. Clark & Oswald, 2010: 5. They add 'these are crucial in supporting emancipatory change'.
42. Baser & Morgan, 2008.
43. G. Morgan, 1997.
44. Anderson & Ackerman Anderson 2001: 3. The implication of such an approach is that facilitating change processes is no longer about 'them' but about 'us' as well. (See as well the Introduction to this volume.)
45. The first three dimensions – content, people, process – may be extracted from the work of Anderson & Ackerman Anderson 2001. The fourth dimension – benefits – has been added by Context, international cooperation in view of the increased results orientation within the development sector.
46. Anderson & Ackerman Anderson, 2001: 136-137.
47. Schein, 1999: 3, 146.
48. Anderson & Ackerman Anderson, 2001: 6-7.
49. See among others: Aldrich, 1999; Ardon *et al*., 2005; De Caluwé & Vermaak, 2002; Thaw, 2002.
50. Anderson & Ackerman Anderson, 2001: 39.
51. See also G. Morgan, 1989: 139-142.
52. G. Morgan, 1989: 140-141.
53. Anderson & Ackerman Anderson, 2001: 32.
54. *Ibid*.
55. The contribution of Lieke Ruijmschoot with regard to this paragraph needs to be acknowledged.
56. Bartczak, 2005; Gubbels & Koss 2000; Johnson & Ludema, 1997; Lusthaus, Adrien, Anderson, & Carden, 2000.
57. I/C Consult, 2002.
58. See: Van der Velden, Leenknegt & Haijtink, 2005: 42-43.
59. Senge, 1990.
60. Anderson & Ackerman Anderson, 2001: 145.
61. The first part of the paragraph is borrowed from Van der Velden, Leenknegt and Haijtink, 2005.
62. James, 1998: 32.
63. *Ibid*., 35-36.
64. Schein, 1999: 19. Italics in the original. 'Unless clients learn to see problems for themselves and think through their own remedies, they will be less likely to implement the solution and less likely to learn how to fix such problems should they occur' (page 18).
65. ECDPM, 2004: 10.
66. *Ibid*., 13.

67. Anderson & Ackerman Anderson, 2001: 152.
68. Champion, Kiel and McLendon, 1985.
69. See Van der Velden, Leenknegt & Haijtink, 2005.
70. See for some early publication about this subject among others Eade, 1997; Bolger, 2000; James, 1998 & 2002; UNDP, 1998; UNDP, 2008; Van der Velden, 2004; Van der Velden & Leenknegt 2006.
71. Lipson & Hunt, 2008; James and Hailey, 2007; IDS bulletin Volume 41, No. 3, 2010. Official agency studies Baser & Morgan, 2008; UNDP, 2006; DAC, 2006; academic writers (Morgan, 2006; Fowler, 2006; Eyben, 2006, Ubels *et al.*, 2010) international NGDOs research (Lipson and Warren, 2006) and action learning from capacity development practitioners (James and Wrigley, 2007).
72. James, 2010.
73. James & Hailey, 2007.
74. The UNDP has defined a similar list of 'Basic principles' (UNDP, 2008).
75. James, 2010: 13–14.
76. Lipson and Warren, 2006.
77. James, 2010: 15.
78. Lipson and Warren, 2006; James, 2010.
79. A few attempts are being made to develop approaches for monitoring and evaluation, these include Roche, 1999 (Chapter 7), Bakewell, 2003, Chapter 10, Engel *et al.*, 2007, UNDP, 2010.
80. Whereby Northern NGDOs have become increasingly like contractors or even subcontractors of multilateral or national donor agencies. (*Ref.* Van der Velden, 2002: 153--154).
81. James, 2010: 18.
82. James, 1998.
83. James, 2010: 19–21. The two boxes have been formulated by Rick James.

Chapter II

Organisational Development and Institutional Development: Case Study Cecoedecon (India)

Staff Members Cecoedecon, Rajasthan (India)

Introduction

The Centre for Community Economics and Development Consultants Society (Cecoedecon) was founded by a group of young social workers to provide relief to flood victims in Jaipur district in 1982. In the 29 years since then the organisation has witnessed many changes in terms of approaches, strategies, programme focus, coverage and organisational ethos.

In 2005, the second phase of the Participatory Initiatives for Integrated Rural Development (PIIRD) was being concluded and a review was conducted with the help of external facilitators. Based on the recommendations of this review team the third phase of the PIIRD was conceived and implemented from April 2006 onwards. This led to one of the major programmes of the organisation, which was supported by a consortium of agencies. In this particular phase, unlike the earlier phases, a new dimension was added in the form of an Organisational Development/Institutional Development (OD/ID) process. Specific initiatives were undertaken to gear the OD/ID process towards systematically improving organisational functions in order to best achieve the vision and mission of Cecoedecon.

From 2006-2010, a series of external and joint reviews have guided the change process in general and Organisational or

Institutional Development in particular. Cecoedecon has undergone a metamorphosis as part of the OD/ID process and seeks to share these experiences with other development actors.

This chapter provides a report of the different transformative events that have allowed the organisation to change, evolve, adapt and develop. Some key chronological events are described in the following pages. The general progression of the meetings and workshops to achieve the goals of the OD/ID process has also been captured. The Appendices recount the various exercises that were carried out at each of these sessions.

Apart from capturing the process, this chapter attempts to convey the emotions of our journey: capture the stories, the excitement, the enthusiasm and even the confusion and fears that were experienced by all of us at Cecoedecon during the process. Quotes from a range of participants who were involved with this process have been included where possible. Cecoedecon hopes that this report will aid other organisations in managing similar changes.

The start of the change process

Right after the external review and the start of the new phase of the programme of PIIRD, talks were held, both officially and unofficially, regarding the meaning of this new concept 'OD/ID'. Many of the staff were discussing it amongst themselves and others were resigned to the fact that this is a change process that they have to now go through.

There were also some who did some Google searching and scanned literature to understand what the OD process meant. This had led to a collection of some literature, which was shared with the staff. These led to the organisation arranging a series of discussions at the branch offices of Cecoedecon.

At the end of these meetings, the conclusion regarding the new concept 'OD/ID' was that it is a change process that has the ability to resolve several problems found within the organisation. At first people were a bit confused and apprehensive about this process.

In the words of Badri Jat, one of the coordinators :

> '*In the staff meeting at Shilki* [training centre of Cecoedecon], *Vermaji and Catherine were both there. They observed the entire meeting and shared their thoughts that the meeting had a few problems: lacking proper preparation, lacking appropriate materials, disruption because of cell phones, people were not projecting their voices and people were not listening, etc. They said that these different problems could be addressed through the medium of OD/ID. They started talking about OD/ID and at that time no one understood what this OD/ID really was.*'

The observation of Giriraj Singh, another coordinator from Malpura, was:

> '*Catherine and Vermaji came to the staff meeting in Malpura* [a branch office] *and they said, 'in addition to the staff meeting today, we will take one hour afterwards to talk about a new subject and do a new exercise. First we sat down in a circle on the floor and we were given the task to write down all the stakeholders of Cecoedecon. One by one, each person had to give an answer. After two rounds, Vermaji said that there still is a stakeholder that is missing...and anyone who can answer will be treated to sweets. Then the group deliberated, but then I answered that we have forgotten the beneficiaries. I won the sweets!*'

During the process of the various staff meetings and exploration of what OD meant, there was a common understanding that changes needed to be effected within the organisation to achieve its mission and vision statements more effectively. There were differing perceptions and also a common feeling that the OD process needed to be facilitated by an external person or team who has a good understanding of the process.

Since Mr. Fons van der Velden from Context, international cooperation, the Netherlands, and Mr. Pradeep Esteves from

Context, India, were involved in the review that had suggested Cecoedecon go through such a process, it was decided to discuss matters with them and take their advice on how to take it forward. Over a period of time, plans firmed up and both Mr. Fons van der Velden and Mr. Pradeep Esteves were asked to facilitate the process and the formal side of that business was taken care of.

Simultaneously, while the external team was being engaged and the initial informal discussions and discussions with the staff at all levels, including the branch offices, were being conducted, the first OD team was formed, consisting of mostly staff from the Cecoedecon central office.

This team started to work on understanding the theoretical concept of OD. As explained earlier, their work was mostly academically oriented and involved scanning the literature which led to an abstract understanding of the concept of OD. This team also wrote a paper that summarised the main ideas about OD as found online and in various publications. However, by practice they soon realised that presenting the theory of OD was creating more confusion than good.

Simultaneously the external facilitators team was being finalised. As the process was creating more confusion, Mr. Fons van der Velden was asked to give advice on how to go forward. Acting on the advice received from the team, the decision was made to switch from abstract theory to a more experience-based process. The external facilitators shared a note titled 'On the golden principles of an OD process'.[1]

> *'Our first team was created to teach others about OD and bring in clarification about its process. With that enthusiasm people started looking at the internet and reviewing the literature to answer the question: what Is OD? After researching and collecting materials on the theory of OD we formulated a paper on OD. Then we went into different field offices to disseminate our findings. When we shared this initial work with the facilitator, he sent us a note, discouraging this process of learning OD from the literature. It is at this time that we received a note from the facilitator on the golden principles of the OD.' (P.M. Paul, Director)*

To assist the transition from an abstract, theoretically-oriented think-tank to a group to guide an experienced-based process, a new 16-member OD team was created based on the selection criteria given below:

- There should be wide diversity in the experience of the team members. This way, the group could take advantage of members with youthful vitality (been with the organisation for 3 to 4 years) and those with aged wisdom (founding members).
- The members should be from many different branch offices, so that the entire organisation can be represented.
- The members should range from all levels within the organisation so that all perspectives and viewpoints are examined. A few examples are: branch heads, unit heads, accountants, driver, representatives of satellite institutions, KSS member, and field workers, etc.
- The members should be devoted to the organisation and its work.

The team was formed after the above criteria were decided internally by Cecoedecon and shared with the external facilitating team. Ms. Neema Pant was selected as the team leader to coordinate the process and also to relate to and work along with the external facilitation team.

In the first few team meetings it was decided that the first task should be a mapping exercise, with which the team would start a comprehensive review of the organisation with the objective to identify and assess the gaps and bottlenecks in Cecoedecon. To accomplish this, the OD team selected 21 documents and these were distributed amongst the members of the OD team. The members reviewed the material and compiled a list of gaps and bottlenecks they felt needed to be addressed.

The documents studied included: reports, annual reports,

mid-term report, gender policies, bilateral meetings minutes, HRD policy, core team retreat, board meeting minutes, branch office reports, workshops, organisational self-assessments, staff monthly meeting minutes, Community Based Organisations (CBOs) registered meetings and external studies.

In addition to the document review staff and members from affiliated and sister organisations such as Kisan Seva Samithi[2], Village Development Committees and colleagues from satellite institutions were interviewed and their opinions with regard to the shortcomings were also captured.

After the review of these various documents and discussions with colleagues, the OD team met and mapped the recurring issues that they had come across and found to be having a negative effect on the functioning of the organisation. These results were shared with the external facilitation team and together it was decided to hold a 'Kick Off workshop', where these findings could be unpacked and understood more deeply as well as develop the next steps as to how these could be overcome.

'Kick Off workshop'

During the OD team meetings the team discussed and developed the content, objectives and the list of participants of the 'Kick Off workshop'. Though the external facilitation team was available in the background it was the team that developed the design of this workshop. Efforts were made to make the level of participation diverse and multidisciplinary. As a result 30 participants from the government, donor agencies, Cecoedecon's partner organisations, and representatives from satellite institutions were invited. Prior to the 'Kick Off workshop', the results of the mapping exercise were shared with all the participants.

The workshop was facilitated by the external facilitation team of Mr. Fons van der Velden and Mr. Pradeep Esteves and the OD team leader Ms. Neema Pant.

The objectives of this workshop were:

- To take stock and recap the status of the process thus far especially in terms of the analysis of the 'root cause' regarding the current organisational status of Cecoedecon.
- To work out the content for the OD process.
- To elaborate on the process as well as define milestones and performance indicators.
- To prepare action plans and to clarify the roles of the various actors such as the OD team, external facilitators, etc.

The workshop was facilitated in a participatory manner whereby all the participants were made to take active part in the process. The participants were first asked to highlight organisational functions which need to be in place in order to best achieve the overall mission of Cecoedecon. Initially the participants highlighted six functional areas that they felt needed to be addressed.

Following the mapping of the functional areas, a gap analysis was done by the participants for each of the functional areas. This was done in different groups after which all the groups got together and discussed the various functional areas and the gaps and prioritised as per the requirements. Ultimately after discussions these five major functional areas were listed by the participants on priority basis:

1. Human Resource Development.
2. Communications.
3. Organisational Learning.
4. Planning, Monitoring and Evaluation.
5. Strategic Decision making.

Comprehensive action plans on how to address the gaps present in these five functions were formulated accordingly.

The methodology adopted during the entire workshop was

enriched by participatory and creative exercises, providing participants space to discuss their innermost thoughts and impressions about the organisation and related issues through focus group discussions and creative presentations, which also kept the energy level of each participant elevated. A very thorough and exhaustive description of the different exercises during the workshop is provided in Appendix B.[3]

There was a general sense of excitement that was felt throughout the workshop, as if a new and somewhat revolutionary change was about to occur. People interviewed years later, who have forgotten the contents of countless other meetings still fondly remember this meeting as being innovative, interesting, useful and even fun. The expression of Shri Krishan Jat, a senior coordinator at Cecoedecon, can be summarised in his own words along with the picture that his team made.

> *'At first I didn't know what OD/ID was, even after I was made a team member of the OD team. I had many questions in my mind, such as, how will we do this? I, along with many staff, felt that there were many problems but we did not know how to progress forward. When the Kick Off workshop happened, everything became clear and we understood the steps we would need to take. In my life, it was the first time I experienced this type of training.*
> *We were given the responsibility of recapping the previous day's meeting. We worked all night long to create a pictorial representation of all that we had learned and accomplished. We made a "thoren dwar".[4] This dwar represented a pathway to accomplish our goals. The Kick Off workshop gave us a path to follow to accomplish our goals. On our illustration we drew stairs leading to the gate, which represented the steps one should take to reach their goals. We were working until 2 in the morning to prepare this. People really liked it and later it was printed out really nicely. After this we became motivated and we really thought that we could implement this.'*

Training of Trainers

Though the team was all excited and eager to start implementing the action plans to overcome the gaps in the five prioritised organisational functions, it was felt that since the OD team members have to play an important role as change agents in the organisation, there was a need to enhance their capacities. With this objective of enhancing the capacities and skills of the change agents a Training of Trainers (ToT) workshop was organised with the support from the external facilitating team.

This workshop provided an opportunity for all the participants to attain clarity and better understanding of the OD process and to also broaden their knowledge on the process as to how to involve all concerned stakeholders towards the achievement of the OD objectives. The ToT workshop was done using a different methodology and to capture this we gladly cite the words of Ms. Sweta Tiwari, the unit head of HRD:

> *'In one of the exercises we were strengthening our listening, summarising and probing skills. In this exercise, one person was given the task of telling a story, while another was told to summarise it and the final was expected to refine the summary. I remember that this activity led to the sharing of many personal stories and experiences, which brought people together. One example was an employee who shared about her past. She talked about how her family and especially her father discouraged her from becoming a chartered accountant, because women in her family typically stayed home. Nevertheless, she persisted with her dream and became an accountant.'*

Mr. Girwar Singh the Branch Manager of Malpura exclaimed:

> *'What I liked most about the ToT workshop was the gallery. The gallery began with the drawing that was presented in the Kick Off workshop followed by a pictorial summary of everything that was accomplished by OD/ID up to this point. This helped clarify many misunderstandings and misconceptions. I also really liked how time was managed. During the ninety-minute sessions, people were intensely involved. Because time was budgeted well, the meetings never went beyond the allotted time.'*

A number of innovative exercises were utilised for this workshop and have been listed in Appendix C for ready reference.

During the process, the participants had also highlighted several 'burning questions' that could serve as focal points for discussions during the ToT. A few of these Burning Questions are listed below:

- How to involve all the organisation staff of Cecoedecon in the OD process, what are the strategies?
- How to bridge the gap between the professional staff and field staff?
- How to ensure the partner community in this process?
- What kind of role will be effective for the partner communities to gain more out of this process?
- How to ensure the maximum reach out of the OD process?
- Whether the projects also come under the purview of the OD process?
- In what way we can learn in this two-day workshop?
- How can I contribute to this OD process?
- I expect to gain something related to administration?
- How can we develop interest and create motivation to the staff on this process?
- What about the documentation of this process?
- How we can sustain this process?
- How can we bridge the gap between the programmes and administration?
- Is it possible to fulfil all the expectations of the participants?
- How can we enhance the skill of OD team?
- To what extent is OD process different from the HR capacity building process?

Board involvement

Since its inception, Cecoedecon has always been privileged with the guidance of able leadership. It is very fortunate to have leadership of such senior and experienced board members. Quarterly board meetings are standard. The progress of the OD process was shared with the board members at every stage so that they could stay abreast of the process and their involvement was ensured. As part of the OD process a board retreat was organised, to review the involvement of the Board in the past, to analyse the present context and to enhance the board's role in future endeavours.

What made the board retreat an especially exciting event was the concept of bringing together so many accomplished leaders and having them sit together to collectively accomplish the various objectives. It is not so often that such a dynamic group, each with their own reservoir of special skills and experiences, can be assembled because most have extremely hectic schedules.

Apart from being organised in a serene place such as Bilochi [an Ayurvedic health resort where the retreat was held], the methodology of the retreat was such that everyone felt involved from the very beginning in the participatory and creative exercises (found in Appendix D). Moreover, the entire process progressed in a relaxed manner aided by the level of enjoyment experienced by the participating Board members who partook in meditation exercises, jokes, songs, and prayers. Conducting an informal get-together provided space for the Board members to get know each other better and to strengthen group solidarity. The external facilitation team along with the OD team leader of Cecoedecon facilitated the retreat.

The commentary of the senior Board members Ms. Bedi and Mr. Bhat capture the mood and process that took place at the board meeting very well. Ms. Bedi described it thus:

> *'What made this event amazing was that very senior members could all sit down and share their experiences. Often with such a*

distinguished group, one finds people unwilling to learn or to open up. But with our group, there was no hesitation to share or learn. The unique aspect of this event was that the trainers did not inundate us with overwhelming amounts of lectures; instead the retreat was very participatory in nature, which I felt was extremely useful and important.'

Mr. Bhat shared that:

'This was an unusual and very good experience. We are all 45 years or older and have entered into a phase of guiding others. Oftentimes it is very difficult to hold such a meeting for board members, because, you know how the saying goes "a doctor is never a good patient". Nevertheless, in this event we became students again and we were all very receptive to this opportunity. The facilitators were very good because they gave us the freedom to search and answer questions by ourselves. This event reinforced the idea that a person can learn at any age. Once again to reiterate, the reason why this event was so unique was because usually in the volunteer sector this sort of meetings never occur and usually board members are unreceptive to become students again. However, these limitations never entered into our meeting.'

The board members then took on various responsibilities and developed a declaration which is popularly known as the Bilochi declaration.[5]

Taking stock: Mid-Term Review

At the midpoint of the PIIRD Phase III programme and the OD/ID process, a Mid-Term Review (MTR) was held to take stock of where the process was leading and whether the effectivity of the programmes had improved and above mentioned 'The Burning Questions' were being addressed.

The specific objectives of the MTR were defined as follows:

1. *Programme Performance*: To assess how effectively the organisation has been able to follow the rights based approach, assess linkages made between micro and macro issues and analyse which policies have been

influenced at various levels.

2. *Organisational Performance*: To review the process initiated under OD/ID process, especially regarding prioritised functions and to assess how far internalisation of the OD/ID has taken place within the organisation.
3. *Linkages*: To review performances of Apex institutions and assess to what extent they have taken over the responsibilities from Cecoedecon to establish linkages for the institutions.

While Mid-Term Reviews are often common in NGDOs and other organisations, what made this a unique and different event was that it was a very inclusive process. Though the process was initiated by Cecoedecon and facilitated by the OD/ID external facilitation team, it was characterised by the participation of various stakeholders. The stakeholders participating were Cecoedecon, staff and leadership, representatives of Board (several formal and informal meetings were held with Board members), representatives of the OD/ID team, representatives of Kisan Seva Samiti Mahasangh (KSSM, farmers union), members of Panchayat Raj Institutions (PRIs, local village councils), donors and other NGDOs and the external consultants of Mid-Term Review.

A methodology was developed that involved all relevant stakeholders truly participating together in all the steps of the review, i.e., the formulation of ToR, preparation of all relevant documents and MTR itinerary, data collection and analysis, report writing as well as debriefing.

In the methodology the emphasis was on collective and individual reflection ('look, learn and listen'), for this purpose the following methods, among others, were among others used: participatory workshops, focus group discussions and 'narratives' (mini story telling exercises).

A core group for the MTR was established consisting of members from Cecoedecon, a representative of the foreign donors, external facilitators and other stakeholders. This core team met daily and reflected whether the MTR process was on track and whether the process met the above-defined parameters.[6]

The Social Return on Investment, popularly known as SROI, is an approach to understanding and managing the impacts of a project, an organisation or a policy. It is based on stakeholders and puts financial values on important impacts, identified by stakeholders, which do not have market values. The aim is to include the values of people that are often excluded from markets in the same terms as used in markets, that is to say money, in order to give people a voice in resource allocation decisions.

Cecoedecon, in collaboration with Context international cooperation, carried out a pilot study on SROI. This pilot study was facilitated by Mr. Peter Das, Mr. Jan Brouwers and Mr. Pradeep Esteves along with a team from Cecoedecon consisting of Mr. P. M. Paul and Ms. Neema Pant. Also included in this study were the Planning Monitoring Evaluation team and members of the KSSM.

Initially a workshop was carried out to provide an understanding of the concepts of SROI and it included a general review of the SROI process followed by a detailed study of local, national and international case studies. Discussions were held on the advantages of SROI, such as valuing the perspectives of the community but also some of the disadvantages such as the inability to standardise SROI because of its reliance on qualitative data gathered from individuals. The workshop ended with an exercise focusing on determining the future steps Cecoedecon could take.[7] As a result, action plans were made based on these future steps. A review of the different activities can be found in Appendix F.

'I have learned many things from these SROI exercises. I and the village community never used to think about the returns on our investments. But from these exercises, we obtained ways to analyse the effectiveness of a variety of programmes that otherwise were

> *difficult to assess. We realised that we do obtain many returns from social projects. For example, we realised the benefits on the work we did on health in Surya and the work we did in Madorajpura on minimum support price. We find this knowledge as valuable as social auditing.*' (Madan Lal Sharma, Treasurer of KSS, Newai).

Civic driven change

In the past few years through working together a relationship between Cecoedecon and Context international cooperation has evolved. Several initiatives have been taken to support the affiliation between the two organisations. One of these initiatives revolved around the concept of Civic Driven Change (CDC). For the last few years, Context international cooperation has been working on the issue of Civic Driven Change at both the conceptual and practical levels.

Cecoedecon and Context are in a process of exploring the possibilities of cooperation with regard to this issue. In line with this, a half-day joint dialogue was organised on June 27, 2008 on the subject of Civic Driven Change with the proactive participation of intellectuals, academicians, and practitioners in the social service sector. The main purpose of the dialogue was to build a common understanding on the rationale of the concept and to share ideas and gather reflections from the participants especially from the context of Indian society.

> '*The concept was very interesting and very new and everyone was very keen to share their concepts of CDC. This was a very unique type of meeting and it was the first time I attended this sort of event. People discussed what our roles will be and also their views on the possible problems that may arise. The first meeting was somewhat difficult for me to grasp because some of the presentations were very technical.*' (Manish Prasad, Unit Head)

As mentioned above, both Cecoedecon and Context were taking the concept of CDC forward jointly. In order to introduce the concept to other stakeholders in Rajasthan and review the applicability of the CDC, a new CDC dialogue was initiated in February 2009 with participation of civil society players who are actively engaged in Rajasthan. About 50 people from various fields attended this dialogue. The main objectives in organising the second dialogue were:

- Review the applicability of CDC approach in the development context in Rajasthan and India.
- Update the participants on latest developments in knowledge and experience of CDC.
- Explore the possibility of a joint action plan.

To accomplish these objectives, in addition to presentations, a number of discussion sessions were conducted with group work. Descriptions on the content of these discussions and group work can be found in Appendix G. Below is an account of the day by Sharad Joshi, founder of Cecoedecon:

> *'Our comments are very much influenced by our mind-sets. NGDOs as well as academicians are wary of new concepts and ways of working. We need to internalise and adapt to new ways of working in order to sustain our commitment to the cause. Unfortunately, the state and the government do not appreciate community led and people led spontaneous initiatives. The case studies that have been shared are very inspiring and have been accomplished by communities without any external support and avoiding propaganda and publicity, and should be appreciated. We also need to become open to change. We need to continue the dialogue on the CDC at different levels and with various stakeholders including policymakers, practitioners, academicians, and also the media. We need to build partnerships and create space for all kinds of opinions.'*

Leadership development programme

To realise and successfully implement the organisational changes brought about by the OD/ID process, especially in relation to Institutional Development, the role and functions of senior leadership becomes crucial. Therefore, with the objective of equipping the existing organisational leadership to cope with a dynamic operating environment, a five-day Leadership

Development Workshop was conducted in March 2009 with 22 key staff members. It was facilitated by Ms. Neema Pant and Ms. Shweta Tiwari from Cecoedecon and Ms. Anne-Marie Schreven and Mr. Fons van der Velden acted as lead facilitators, aided by a ten-member steering committee that acted as a sounding board and monitored the progress of the workshop.

The workshop was seen as an opportunity to define the context and organisational and individual leadership functions, to identify key leadership skills required. This also offered an occasion to understand the organisation's existing culture and to identify how a leader should operate within that culture and to assess the opportunities and implications for the future role of the organisation. To make the workshop as innovative, memorable, exciting and as interesting as possible, a number of exercises were conducted which are listed in Appendix G.

Specifically, exercises undertaken across the five-day workshop identified that trust and listening are key leadership skills. Trust, especially mutual trust, is inherently linked to organisational success as it elevates the commitment of the organisation's members and sustains efforts with minimal need for management control and monitoring.

Listening was divided into three key categories; 'listening for the head', 'listening for the heart' and 'listening for the feet'. It was identified that each member has to strive to operate more effectively at each level of listening and to also express himself or herself at each level of listening. It was also identified that the culture of an organisation is critical to help foster and develop key leadership skills. The leaders in conjunction with the members have the responsibility to help direct and shape a healthy and dynamic culture in the organisation. Below is a paraphrased testimonial of Govind Narayan Vijay, unit head:

> *'In one exercise, we were paired into groups. One person wore a blindfold while the other was allowed to see. Our objective was to reach a room far away and there were many obstacles in our way such as stairs. The person without a blindfold had to navigate the other to reach the destination. This taught us how to use teamwork*

to accomplish a goal. It was also a trust building exercise. In another exercise, we wrote down our good and bad qualities. This sort of self-evaluation, followed by discussion was helpful. I remember that Bauwarji was next to me and he admitted that he was often easily angered. He even made the commitment that he would change; however, he also remarked that people should realise how busy he can become.'

Outcomes of the OD/ID process

The primary objective of this chapter has been to provide a view on the OD/ID process independent of our organisation. For this reason we have provided detailed descriptions of our exercises but have refrained from providing an exhaustive account of Cecoedecon's accomplishments. Nevertheless, this last section is devoted to the general benefits that we have observed, so that the usefulness of this process can be understood.

Integration of OD into systems

Cecoedecon has established itself as a learning organisation. Over the years, the organisation has faced significant levels of change including organisational growth, organisational restructuring, a greater emphasis on partnership building, a changing role of the organisation and hence the changing role of individual staff. Being a learning organisation, the organisation has adopted and integrated the outcomes of the OD process into the system and procedures of the organisation and thus far, has successfully managed to adopt changes at different levels of the organisation.

Initiatives taken at the organisational level

At the organisational level various efforts like programme reviews, leadership development training, policy dissemination, etc., were embarked upon for enhancement of strong organisational systems.

Managing the changing role

With the adoption of the facilitation mode of operation there were certain obvious changes in the role of individual staff. Now their responsibilities were more facilitation-oriented, however, the role of implementer also still continued for individual staff.[8]

Positioning of staff in the new organisational structure

With the change in the organisational precedence came a change in the organisational structure and, therefore, in the positions of individual staff. While we were proposing the new organisational structure we involved all the staff in the process.

Intensive exercises were done in the staff meetings and core team meeting to finalise the new organisational structure. The proposed organisational structure could have fostered some resistance and discontent among some of the staff members, however, because we planned the change carefully, this was avoided for the most part. The staff members were given an open choice in selecting the thematic area of their interest and also the position on which they wanted to work. This was followed by an interaction between staff and management in which they were given a chance to reflect upon their competencies and skills.

Communication

Effective communication is the foundation of the effectiveness and success of any organisation. Therefore, ensuring transparency and precision in communication is fostered in the operational culture of Cecoedecon.

There are continuous efforts to ascertain that downward communication, upward communication and communication of supervisor with his/her team take place in healthy and informative manner. It is also considered imperative that values and organisational concepts should be transmitted from the old staff members to the newly joined staff. Cecoedecon is characterised by a diversified workforce—there are staff who are working from its inception along with those who are very new. They are the witness of critical times and various achievements of the organisation. Despite having a limited education they feel and understand the pulse of the community at the grass roots level.

Interface between new staff and management

A new entrant in an organisation is often full of apprehensions, curiosity, anxiety and hesitation and has a number of questions. If these questions are answered to a person's satisfaction and are resolved in a timely manner and their aspirations are well managed then there are better chances that this will translate into a long working relationship. Therefore, the leadership of an organisation plays a crucial role in shaping the experience, perception and managing the expectations of new staff members. Moreover, new staff often looks to the leaders as their role models of what is desired from staff members in the organisation. Therefore, meetings between management and new staff are organised at regular intervals as an attempt to establish a learning interface between these persons. These meetings are prepared in the style of a forum through which new staff could share theii feelings, expectations and experience with the management staff. This was also seen as an opportunity to understand the culture of the organisation by new staff members.

Organisational learning

Learning is a continuous process that integrates ideas and actions. It provides a link between past and future, requiring us to look at the meaning and intentions behind our actions. Learning enriches what we do as an individual and collectively as an organisation. It is central to organisational effectiveness in developing the quality of our work and organisational relevance, adaptability, innovation and sustainability. Therefore, significant efforts have been undertaken to strengthen the process of organisational learning. Sharing of learning experiences from an individual level to an organisational level has been ensured by each of the staff members. Staff meetings of all the staff and branch staff meetings are the forums in which the learnings through different trainings, workshops and exposures were shared with remaining staff. The practice of applying the experiences and outcomes from one project to other projects within the organisation has also been adopted as a result of this process.

Adaptation of lessons in the Institutional Development process

Partnership is intended to promote joint problem solving, resource exchange, cooperation, coordination and coalition building. Sincere efforts have been made to work on the strengthening of organisational partnerships at different levels. In the coming project phase this style of partnership has been taken up as the underlying process for Institutional Development. Institutional Development is being carried out at two levels. One is the development of village level organisations, CBOs and People's Institutions as institutions and the other is the positioning of Cecoedecon in relation to other civil society institutions.

At both of these levels partnership is the underlying process through which lessons learnt and experiences of Cecoedecon are consolidated and shared with larger civil society. Partnership building brings together institutional capabilities and human resources in the form of skills, experiences and ideas for taking up issues that are beyond the control of a single organisation.

The lessons from the OD process in terms of formalising the procedures have been adopted in the Institutional Development process. Establishing KSS Mahasangh as a separate entity, vision building exercise for KSS, ensuring clarity in their roles providing training that strengthened their internal systems were among the various efforts taken to improve institutional development with regard to the village level organisations.

There was a deeply felt realisation that at the global and national level only collective voices and actions taken jointly by civil society would be able to contribute positive change to the life of the community. Cecoedecon wanted to contribute in facilitating the process of building an enabling environment for civil society actors so that they are able to raise collective voices. In view of a rapidly changing context there was a need to strengthen the civil society movement, especially in the State of Rajasthan. It was felt strongly that Cecoedecon should take a leading role in bringing the issues to the fore so that discussions could be generated on aid effectiveness, interface between civil society and governance and the obstacles civil society encounters in forwarding their agenda. Additionally, civil society should be engaged to collectively take similar actions.

Taking the initiatives forward, a network was established at the State level and called '*Sajha Manch*'.[9] The members of this network are the representatives of some of the leading NGDOs of Rajasthan. The network aims to achieve the objective of taking up emerging issues like climate change, economic justice, biodiversity, etc., and to work together to solve the problems that result from these.

Finally, presented below are two contrasting testimonials. In one testimonial we see that the OD/ID process can be a difficult one, especially at the initial stages. Persistence and a desire to change are the key factors that allow an organisation to overcome the many obstacles that present themselves. The second testimonial captures the positive development that a properly implemented OD/ID process can have on an individual.

> *'In front of our funding agency and core team we gave a presentation on the progress of our programme. The external facilitators had already known everything that we had accomplished at Cecoedecon. So when they heard our*

presentation, they were somewhat disappointed because we were unable to convey everything that we had done.' (Badri Jat, coordinator).

'A very large hunger mapping exercise was conducted in which nine NGOs independently worked on topics such as public distribution systems, hunger death prevention and livelihoods. At the end, all the NGOs came together in a large meeting in Bhopal where they presented all of their findings. Many people gave presentations, most of which were highly educated. I was not that educated but after giving my presentation I remember people congratulating me on the effectiveness of my work; they said it was the best one there. I found out later that a former employee of Cecoedecon (that moved to a different NGO) told the director that he saw great capacity building in me and that he noticed a very significant change. I feel that this was accomplished because of the OD process.' (Chitterji, Unit Head).

REFERENCES

1. The golden principles are attached as Appendix 'A' with this chapter.
2. Farmers union.
3. For more information on the 'Kick Off workshop' a separate report on the workshop is available upon request from Cecoedecon.
4. A decorated and auspicious door — when a marriage is sealed, a new relationship is created and the husband and wife walk through this gate.
5. The details of the board retreat can be found in the detailed report of the event which is available upon request from Cecoedecon.
6. A detailed report on the process and outcomes of this process is available from Cecoedecon.
7. A detailed report on the pilot study conducted at Cecoedecon is available upon request from Cecoedecon.
8. The different roles that can be played by an organisation such as Cecoedecon are elaborated in Chapter I in the section 'The role of relative outsiders'.
9. Which means 'in cooperation with other people'.

Annexure 'A': The Golden Rules

1. Need to demystify OD

While engaging in a process of Organisational Change such as within Cecoedecon it is important not to start at a theoretical level, but with a practical approach and exercise. Organisational Development and Organisational change is part and parcel of Cecoedecon's organisational evolution, hence nothing special or new that needs to be demystified. Hence, it is suggested not to start with theoretical explanations, articles, etc., but with a much more practical and down to earth approach. The only thing that makes the present process a bit special is that organisational change will be a bit more systematic and consciously positioned on the agenda of Cecoedecon and the people's organisations.

2. Cecoedecon in the driver's seat

As such a process should be demand driven, what is the demand Cecoedecon has or what are the areas Cecoedecon wants to work on? Where is the scope for improvement? What are the issues that staff members of Cecoedecon are struggling with? What goes well and can be expanded? There is a preliminary agenda as a result of the Organisational self-assessment workshop, which was carried out as per the external evaluation of PIIRD-II programme, but is it relevant if we do not serve the needs of people? We should respond to people's demands and it takes time to analyse what it is that they need and what makes them happy.

3. Role of external facilitators

The ownership of the process lies with Cecoedecon. Cecoedecon should be in the driver's seat. The external facilitators cannot help Cecoedecon. They can only help Cecoedecon to help itself.

4. Organisational growth

Where there is growth, there are growing pains. There will be joy and pain. It may sometimes be difficult to let old things go, and sometimes there will be insecurity and uncertainty. It is good that people are having apprehensions about the suggested process. It means that staff members of Cecoedecon understand what they are facing. We need to keep in mind that Cecoedecon is there to serve the poor and marginalised. It is more important to keep that in mind than to gain conceptual clarity on OD.

5. Building on existing capacities

We have to build on what is there in the organisation: capacities, experience, documents. A starting point is to appreciate and value what is already there within Cecoedecon and people's organisation. Then jointly see what else we need to do.

Annexure 'B': Exercises and Schedules of the 'Kick Off Workshop'

Day 1: Inauguration

The workshop was inaugurated with a short yoga exercise for 10 minutes to give the participants that extra bit of energy to bring up the level of concentration among the participants. To symbolise the 25 years of working of the organisation, 25 candles were lit by participants. After a brief round of introduction Mr. P.M. Paul welcomed the participants with a special mention for Mr. Fons van der Velden and Mr. Pradeep Esteves. Mr. Paul provided a brief background of the organisation mentioning how it has developed since inception, focusing on how the organisation has grown. After sharing the major objectives of the workshop, some time was devoted to focusing on the methodologies to be adopted for the workshop that was to be facilitated by the facilitators, namely:

- Participatory group task and creative exercise;
- Focused Group Discussion (FGD); and
- Different creative exercise.

Mr. Fons van der Velden then threw some light on the various parameters stating how we (Cecoedecon) have adapted to the changes in the context of the review in 2005 and that the major role will be played by the participants of Cecoedecon only. The parameters discussed were:

- Vision, mission, principles and strategy of Cecoedecon are not to be redefined.

- Cecoedecon will be in the driver's seat: OD team.
- Limited role of external facilitator.
- An OD exercise is part of natural growth process with objective to realise the dreams of the organisation.
- Building on existing experience and capabilities, and sometimes being challenged to go beyond the comfort zone.

Exercise 1: Hope, fear and question

The facilitators at the start of the first exercise of the workshop set the tone for the coming days and asked every participant to write down their hopes, fears and questions on three different pieces of paper, keeping in view these two learning questions:

1. What do I bring to the meeting terms of 'Hopes and Fears'?
2. If I could have one question in relation to the OD of Cecoedecon answered by this workshop what would the question be?

Exercise 2: Image of the organisation

This exercise was designed to determine what image the participants have of Cecoedecon and how they perceive it has grown since its inception with respect to its characteristics. Mr. Fons van der Velden explained the exercise to the participants and every participant was asked to make a drawing depicting the organisational image and just show the picture to one another and try to comprehend the picture and the sense behind it. Then form a group of 4–5 people and try to make a bigger picture with consensus and it also can be picture within the picture or a story within the story if a consensus is not there within the group.

Exercise 3: Mind mapping to encapsulate the important functions the organisation needs to perform in order to achieve its mission

To further unfold the images made by each participant and their respective groups in the previous exercise, a mind mapping exercises was done. The main purpose was to let the participants express the thought patterns, pictures and associations that already existed in their mind. The participants were asked to draw a diagram again depicting the principal thought or idea (i.e., the vision, mission and strategy of Cecoedecon) in the centre of a blank page with major branches, representing connected themes, radiating out from the centre. Second and third levels of thought, expressed in key words or images, are connected to the main branches with thinner lines.

Exercise 4: Participatory stakeholder analysis of Cecoedecon OD trajectory

This was the last exercise for the day and designed to achieve an exhaustive list of the different stakeholders who will be directly and indirectly related to the important functions that were narrowed down in the previous exercise. Mr. Pradeep Esteves explained the exercise for the groups. Participants were divided in four groups and every group had to present a small play and the other groups had to identify the different stakeholders involved/mentioned in the play/skit.

Day 2

The second day activities started with a brief recap of the previous day's work by Mr. Paul. Mr. Pradeep Esteves shared the outcome, specific observations and decisions taken by the steering committee meeting that met late on the first day:

- No Session will be more than 90 minutes.
- The concept of *Chupa Rustam* — a box — was introduced and the participants were asked to write

down any question or suggestion that they might hesitate to ask openly and put it in the box to be dealt with during the workshop.

Mr. Fons van der Velden set the following agenda for the second day:

- Finalisation of Code of Conduct for the entire OD process (principles and values).
- Completion of analysis of stakeholders involved.
- Self-assessment of the present organisational functions of Cecoedecon.

Exercise 5: Stakeholder analysis: Analysis of interest and power

Introducing the first exercise for the day, which was a continuation of the exercise from the previous day, which was carried out to determine the interest and power of the stakeholders in our organisational overview, Mr. Pradeep Esteves divided the participants into six groups and asked them to make a matrix to explain interest and power of stakeholders. The matrix was divided into four quadrants depicting:

- *High interest and high power*: The stakeholders, who have high interest in the organisation and also enjoy the power to influence the decisions.
- *High interest and low power*: The stakeholders, who have high interest in the organisation but do not have power to influence the decisions.
- *Low interest and high power*: The stakeholders, who have low interest in the organisation but enjoy high power to influence the decisions.
- *Low interest and low power*: the stakeholders, who have low interest in the organisation and also do not have power to influence the decisions.

Initially the exercise was quite difficult to understand, and

Mr. Fons van der Velden explained it using the example of a family to help the participants understand the exercise. He stated there are various members in a family: parents, children, friends, relatives, etc., but all the members do not enjoy equal level of power and interest, some have a high interest and also power to influence the family decisions, some have a high interest and no power and some of them do not have power or interest. Cecoedecon (or for that matter any organisation) can be perceived as a family and stakeholders are members of this family. Think of Cecoedecon as a family and place stakeholders on matrix with respect to their interest and power.

Exercise 6: Code of Conduct

What should be the principles and values, which are taken as the basis for the OD process? An exercise on code of conduct was designed to lay down the values and principles that the different stakeholders need to apply in order to execute the functions in a most efficient manner so as to build upon the existing organisational characteristics. Exercise started with two participants working together to identify three important principles and values, then two pairs to merge and make groups of fours and identified three most significant principles and values amongst the six (identified principles by both group of two participant). Again repeat this process, with two groups merging to form groups of eight and identify the three most important values and principles according to the perceptions and consensus in the group.

After that discussion, participants made some suggestions: suggesting that space is required to make OD process successful as it is a continuous process, hence, resources are also required for its continuity so there should be a principle 'space for continuity', participation should be inclusive, equity principle should be included, space for agreement/disagreement, difference between acceptance and approval, it should be ensured that every person gets equal opportunities for participation and they should comply to agreement and keep in mind that acceptance is not always approval.

Exercise 7: Mapping exercise by OD team

The OD team has done some preparatory work for the process; one of them was to review the already existing documents of the organisation and to identify crucial issues related to OD. Ms. Neema Pant did the presentation of that mapping exercise.

Exercise 8: Self-Assessment of organisational functions

After one and a half days of work it was time to achieve more clarity for ourselves regarding the functions that came up on the first day and to assess that how important these functions are. Why we feel that these functions are important? And at the same time what is the scope of opportunity for improvement with respect to these functions. Mr. Fons van der Velden added one more function – leadership – to the list. According to him, leadership is a one of the most important organisational functions and it is related to almost every person. Leadership means: to coach people, to support them and motivate them. Participants were divided into five groups and each group was given two functions to analyse on the following basis:

1. To what extent are these functions at present fulfilled within Cecoedecon and more in particular how do you value the present quality (on the scale of: excellent, good, moderate, bad, very bad) and why?
2. What do you consider to be one priority area for this OD process and why?

Exercise 9: OD priorities

Five groups were formed and participants were given the document and asked to follow the procedure as follows:

- Read the Document (Mapping Exercise by OD team).
- Do you want to add one or more priorities?
- Or do you want to elaborate or modify one of the OD priorities that is already on the list?

After listing of the priority areas, discussion was held among the participants. After that, votes were cast by participants to decide upon OD priorities. Every person was supposed to cast three votes but only two votes could be cast for one priority area.

Day 3

The third day started with a quick reflection of the previous day's work by Mr. Jat in a very innovative manner by using a diagram (that summed up the theme of OD process), and that was appreciated by all.

After that questions and suggestions were invited from the participants to review previous day activities. Some questions/ suggestions that came up were:

(a) What is the purpose of matrix exercise?
(b) Participants were supposed to take care of guiding principle and values while they were dealing with priority area, but this was missing it seemed.
(c) Change is very natural in Organisation/Staff's behaviour during OD process, what could be the behavioural change that can negativeiy affect the OD process? (Inputs from facilitators.)
(d) The theoretical part should be included to enhance understanding (conceptual level).

Mr. Fons van der Velden replied, paraphrasing Rainer Maria Rilke[1] that 'sometimes it is good to live with question to understand it deeply/clearly rather than having a quick spontaneous answer. In the course of time one definitely gets the answer'. Mr. Fons van der Velden put forward the day as 'day to consolidate all that we have done'. He also explained the various dimensions of OD in plain words.

Exercise 10: Fear, hope and question

Participants were asked to take back the Hope, Fear and Questions that they had written and discuss with someone in the group so as to judge to what extent these expectations have been realised and why? And what do you take away as the major learning from this workshop in view of the learning question. Participants were given five minutes to discuss this with their neighbours and share (the feelings) with the participants on board.

REFERENCE

1. '...I would like to beg you dear Sir, as well as I can, to have patience with everything unresolved in your heart and to try to love the questions themselves as if they were locked rooms or books written in a very foreign language. Don't search for the answers, which could not be given to you now, because you would not be able to live them. And the point is to live everything. Live the questions now. Perhaps then, some day far in the future, you will gradually, without even noticing it, live your way into the answer'. (Rilke, 2000) (Published in originally 1903).

Annexure 'C': Trainer of Trainers Workshop

Mr. Fons van der Velden started the session by expressing warm greetings to all the participants to the workshop on behalf of the OD core team and workshop facilitators. Before embark on the exercises he requested all participants to introduce themselves with their roles and responsibilities within the organisation and he also asked them to make known any burning question in their mind regarding the OD process. All participants responded as well as adding to the list of burning questions.

After completion of the participants' introductions, stating their roles and responsibilities and their burning question regarding the OD process, Mr. van der Velden introduced himself. Following his introduction, he explained the purpose of using questions as a tool and involving the participants in raising burning questions. He explained that the purpose is not to give immediate answers but to draw the participants into the search for solutions and to carry it over towards the process.

The session progressed with the announcement of the purpose, agenda and methodology of the workshop by Mr. Fons van der Velden.

Agenda	*Purpose*	*Methodology*
DAY ONE • Sharing of information on OD activities. • Enhance capacities of the stakeholders. Day TWO • Roles and responsibilities of the stakeholders at different levels. • Formulation of measurement system of the process.	• Share the activities carried out. • Enhance capacities of the stakeholders. • Attain clarity about the OD process. • Develop system of measurements. • Frame action plan and follow-up.	• Participatory group tasks. • Creative exercises. • Focus group discussion. • Session with flexible approach.

Exercise 1: Client–Consultant

Before the start of this exercise, Mr. Fons van der Velden gave instructions about the exercise which required the participants to sit face to face and achieve eye contact. He then directed them to play the role of the client and consultant.

The idea behind this exercise is to:

- Discover the capacity of the stakeholder to chart out the problems and doubts regarding the OD process.
- Generate new ideas and solutions.
- Build the capacity for sharing the information.
- Develop more understanding of the process.
- Provide opportunity to the stakeholders to bring forward solutions for different problems.

Firstly the OD team members played the consultant role and the other participants played the role of client. A maximum of 5 minutes was given to each position and the participants (i.e., clients) were asked to raise doubts/questions/problems towards the OD team members (i.e., consultants) and OD team to give solutions and suggestions as a response. Then after 5-6 shifts the roles were interchanged and the clients acted as a consultant and the consultants acted the role of client.

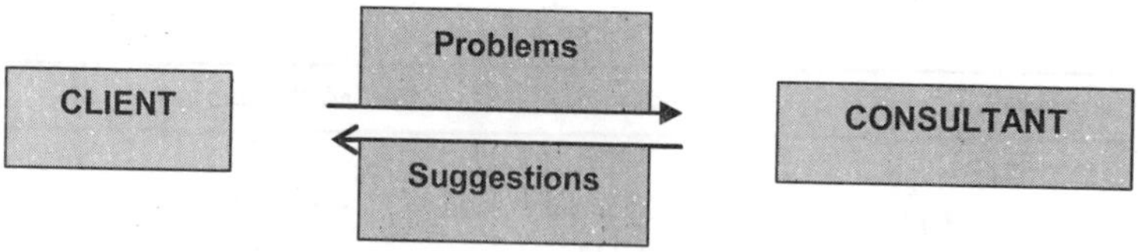

Schematic Representation

Exercise 2: Whispering communication exercise

The purpose of this exercise was to demonstrate the change in the content of a message conveyed by passing it through several members by ear-to-ear communication. Mr. Fons van der

Velden asked Ms. Neema Pant to start the whispering communication process with a message. The message was communicated by whispering the message close to the recipient's ear. The message passed on through 10 participants and then the message was announced out loud by the person at the end. Now it was possible to assess the level communication efficiency. Only 40 per cent of the message that reached to the end point was correct when compared to the message at the starting point.

Exercise 3: Listening, Summarising and Probing (LSP)

The participants were divided into groups of 3 members each to carry on the exercise. The three members in the group were given different roles. The roles were: (1) storyteller; (2) summariser; (3) referee.

Mr. Fons van der Velden gave the set of instructions:

- One member has to tell the story.
- There should be no interruption during the telling of the story.
- Apart from the storyteller the remaining two members should actively listen to the story.
- After completion of the story the summariser has to summarise it.
- After the summarisation the referee has to amplify/correct it if there is any mistake/deviation in the content of summary compared to the story delivered by the storyteller.
- Finally all three members in a group have to work together to bring out the main message of the story.

Exercise 4: Exercise on reading, observing and distilling essence

The purpose of this exercise was to enhance the capacity of the participants in the line of reading/observing, distilling facts, extracting the excerpt /essence /extract of the proceedings.

This particular exercise differs somewhat from the other exercises. The exercise is carried out by the participants outdoors. Again the participants were broken into groups of three each to carry out the exercise. The three members in the group have different roles. The instructions for this exercise are:

- Identify a tree by each group.
- *Parts*: Make your close observation of the different parts of the tree (e.g., Colour, Texture, size of the various parts of the tree. Do not discuss with each other at the time of observation. Record the fact as a fact.
- *Whole*: Next observe the tree from a distance individually to get the overall shape of the tree (i.e., gesture of the tree). What image comes to your mind? What does your imagination say? Record it.
- Share your whole and parts observations with the group members.
- *Essence*: Distil the essence from your observations.
- Incorporate your imagination in your creative poem.

Annexure 'D': Board Retreat

Exercise 1: Rediscovering the motivation

Assorted experiences were shared by the Board members. Every Board member contributed enriching experiences, skills and knowledge pertinent to their area of specialisation.

Exercise 2: Past performances

This exercise was an appreciative enquiry on the past performance of the Board with respect to what has gone well, what needs to be done more and what could have been done differently. A list was made of the results of this brainstorming session.

Exercise 3: Contextual analysis

After a brief presentation on the 25 years of work at Cecoedecon, the next exercise was on scanning the development context. While scanning the present development context through a brainstorming exercise, a variety of social, cultural and economic issues came up. These issues were discussed further and then categorised.

Exercise 4: Visioning exercise

It was clarified that this exercise was not to change the existing vision of Cecoedecon but rather to get an idea from the current context of what the Board's involvement could be. The Board members were requested to draw a picture envisioning

Cecoedecon in the year 2015. A common future identity was obtained from this.

Exercise 5: Mapping exercise

Taking the outcomes of all the previous exercises and with analysis of the past performance of the Board, the members outlined the Board's roles and responsibilities.

Exercise 6: Character of the Cecoedecon Board

This exercise was to define the core characteristics of Cecoedecon's Board. Three different statements were extracted from the exercises which were later converged into one.

Exercise 7: Concluding exercises

At the end of the retreat, the Board members presented a draft declaration. There was a brief discussion on the same; the discussion concluded with an agreement that the subcommittee would continue to work on the declaration and circulate it for suggestions. The Board members also worked out individual action plans, which included sharing the experience of the retreat with their colleagues, lending support in report writing, visiting the field, interacting with Cecoedecon staff, translating learning into practice and working with the Human Resources unit of Cecoedecon for capacity enhancement.

Annexure 'E': SROI Workshop[1]

Exercise 1: Review of SRoI

The first day of the workshop consisted of walking through the gallery (exhibition) of the Social Return on Investment (SRoI) process in Cecoedecon. This reiterated the meaning of SRoI while also providing a general review of actions taken. This gallery presented glimpses of the building blocks of SRoI including the introductory workshop on SRoI, briefs on the case studies undertaken by Cecoedecon, experiences of training of trainers organised by Context, international cooperation in the Netherlands and SRoI in the new Forward Plan of Cecoedecon.

Exercise 2: Study of local case studies

The visit to the gallery set the tone and discussion was carried forward by the detailed presentation of case studies on SRoI undertaken by Cecoedecon. In total, three case studies were shared. The first case study was of Jevali village in Newai block. The issue in this case was the social return on investment of an anicut.[12] The second was valuing the social return on investment of an alternative centre in the village Chawandiay Bagriyan of Malpura block. The third case was the social return on investment of Crèche Centre in Garurwasi village.

The presentation of cases generated discussions on issues such as monetisation and how it is not possible to monetise everything. It was also discussed that SRoI is a time-intensive exercise and preparation or homework is required before undertaking the cases. More discussions were given on the topics of: timely and proper dissemination of information to the community, availability and use of secondary data to obtain more accurate SRoI ratios. From this workshop, one of the strengths of SRoI emerged: that people's perspectives are taken into account.

Exercise 3: Study of case studies from far away

The afternoon session began with sharing of experiences from other parts of the world. A case study of the Tanzanian milk processing industry was examined, as well as a case study of apple growers in Himalayan region. All of this experience sharing and these case study presentations led to an understanding that there is a need to enhance capacity of the community in using this tool as well as a need to define the scope of the SRoI exercise. It was also understood that the SRoI ratio would be different for different areas of work so it cannot be standardised.

Exercise 4: Future of Cecoedecon

The second day of the workshop was on future planning of Cecoedecon with regard to SRoI. Some groups suggested taking the SRoI process up further in a joint venture by Cecoedecon and Context, international cooperation as to achieve this capacity building of community and staff should be done, dissemination of learning with other stakeholders should be integral part of future action and to bring more clarity regular practice is required.

REFERENCES

1. Brouwers *et al.*, 2010 provides an introduction into the SROI approach and methodology.
2. A dam or mole made in the course of a stream for the purpose of regulating the flow of a system of irrigation.

Annexure 'F': Civic Driven Change Dialogue

Exercise 1: Buzz discussions

The participants were requested to get into a buzz group discussion about the following two questions:

- Where are we in terms of our understanding on CDC ?
- What are the areas that need to be explored further?

Exercise 2: Group work

The discussion was followed by group work where four groups were given certain questions to consider, then put their answers on the flip chart and placed it in the gallery for other participants and facilitators to refer to:

- How does the CDC philosophy and approach relate to your own work/experience?
- What issues related to the CDC need to be explored further?
- What suggestions do you have for a joint action plan?
- What can you contribute to a further exploration of the CDC?

All the groups put up their flip charts in the gallery and the facilitator invited the participants to review them. After lunch focus group discussion was organised in which the facilitator asked participants to consider certain questions:

- What inspired you? What struck you?

- What issues do you want to take forward? What do we need to take forward?
- What can we, as individuals and organisations, contribute to a follow up?

Annexure 'G': Leadership Development Workshop

Exercise 1: Understanding leadership

The group work was started off with a mind mapping exercise to identify the external and internal changes that influence the performance of the leaders within the organisation. This exercise was followed up with an exercise to identify the leadership functions required to combat and manage the external and internal changes. The exercise was capped off with identifying, by using only nouns and verbs, the leadership qualities required by the leaders to fulfil the necessary leadership functions.

Exercise 2: Trust and listening

The members of the workshop were divided into pairs and in each pair one was designated as leader and the other as a follower and blindfolded. Next the leader was told to guide the blindfolded follower achieve a certain task within a certain time limit. The goal of the exercise was for the leaders to realise their responsibilities, gain the trust of their followers and successfully guide them towards the goal.

This exercise revealed the importance of listening and the different levels of listening that a leader should possess. Listening with the brain involves facts and figures; listening with the heart implies emotions and feelings; listening with the feet individuates the intention and agenda with which one speaks. The leader and the follower are required to have and develop all three levels of listening.

Two different exercises were conducted on listening. The first involved the members of the workshop being divided into groups of three to undertake each level of listening. The groups struggled with 'listening with the feet' and this part of the exercise was postponed to the following day. The second involved a 15-minute exercise where the leaders were encouraged to listen to and gain knowledge from the senior staff members. The environment, energy level, high spirits, values and culture gave members an opportunity to learn about what inspired their colleagues.

Exercise 3: Organisational leadership

In order to develop a better understanding of the functions of different organisational leadership roles an exercise was undertaken to define the functions of 'implementer', 'facilitator', 'manager' and 'leader' through various group exercises.

Exercise 4: Leadership competencies and skills

One of the facilitators facilitated a group work exercise to distinguish competencies and skills. Competency is defined as a combination of knowledge, skills and behaviour that an employee needs to possess in order to perform functions of a job position that contribute to successful performance. Skills are defined as individual qualities/proficiencies that are helpful for a specific task or job.

A second exercise was undertaken to distinguish between the competencies and skills characterised for different roles within Cecoedecon (Leader, Manager, Facilitator and Implementer). The outcome of the exercise is shown in the Table below:

Role	*Competencies*	*Skills*
Leader	Knowledgeable, honest, motivator, decision making power, patience, farsightedness, build relationships	Listener, guidance, team spirit, realise the needs of the team, change according to the context
Manager	Control over systems, follow up, coordination	Administrator, time management, analytical skills, focused, interpersonal skills, problem solving
Facilitator	Patience, innovative, build and maintain relationships, committed, good observer	Good listener, mentor, ability to guide, distillation skills, motivator
Implementer	Planning, utilise resources, technical knowledge	Time management, mobiles resources, interpersonal skills.

Exercise 5: Wrap up exercise

On the last day of the workshop, the participants were asked to rethink the questions concerning personal leadership they had expressed on the first day of the workshop. All of the participants modified their questions which was an indication that the workshop had been successful in understanding and improving leadership qualities, improving their communication skills and gaining increased confidence.

The exercise was then linked to the organisational level and efforts were taken to relate these to the functions of the organisation in its changing context.

Participants were also asked to give individual feedback in one word on how they felt after attending the workshop. Accordingly comments like ‘good’, ‘confident’, ‘enriched’ and ‘happy’ were received from the participants.

Chapter III

Learning in Development Organisations;

Some Reflections about the Relationship between the Dutch Government and Civil Society Organisations in the Netherlands[1]

Fons van der Velden and *Sarah Cummings*

Background

As part of the discussion of the learning capacity of development organisations in North and South, in this chapter the focus is specifically on learning in the context of the relationship between the Dutch Government and civil society organisations in the Netherlands.

Introduction

From the early 1990s onwards there has been a growing realisation that organisational effectiveness is correlated with an ability to learn from experience.[2] This innovative insight, which now strikes us as blindingly obvious, is of particular relevance to the development sector. Ostensibly dedicated to social political change, development organisations predominantly function as natural open systems, where performance is very dependent on and sensitive to instability and rapid change in the external environment.[3] Moreover, poor accountability — and for that matter a limited learning capacity — has affected the credibility and legitimacy of organisations.

Until very recently, 'learn and adapt' capacity received very little attention within development organisations in both North and South. As far back as 1993, Smillie and Helmich observed that development is, or should be, a knowledge-based endeavour, something echoed by many other commentators since then. The importance of learning what works, and why, is essential to success. Knowing what does not work might even be more essential.[4] The authors regretfully observe that the 'failure to learn from failure' is most probably one of the greatest shortcomings of the development sector. Such situations are, as recent developments show, common in North and South, East and West.[5]

The challenge of complexity

Almost one and a half decade ago, Robert Chambers made specific reference to 'chaos and complexity theory' while surveying alternative ideas.[6] Now-a-days, it is received wisdom that development can have different characteristics varying from rather simple to complicated, complex and chaotic processes and a combination of those and is in general a non-linear process.[7]

Despite this greater realisation, this understanding has not always been put into practice; policies, instruments and procedures within the development sector are quite often based on contemporary versions of the modernisation theory and too often based on the assumption that development can be seen as a rather linear process. Manifestation of this is the spread of the Logical Framework Approach (LFA) within the development sector, almost as a 'mono-culture'. Rihani puts it succinctly: 'Under these conditions, rigid plans and policies are inappropriate'.[8] This has implications for learning and we will deal with this point further below.

Knowledge and diversity

It is now accepted wisdom in the development sector that people ('stakeholders') may have different perceptions of the same situation or 'reality'. Reality in a dynamic universe is non-objective. Indeed, consciousness is the only reality. Situations can be viewed from different perspectives, each of which is equally legitimate and real to the respective groups of participants. This can be described as the perspective of multiple realities.

Even more fundamental, is not only how organisations deal with their own knowledge and learning internally, but also how Southern partners are included in these initiatives. Ironically, when Southern partners are included, knowledge benefits most often accrue to the donor or development organisation rather than to the Southern partners. The participation of these partners is often instrumental rather than driven by effective participation of all stakeholders in the development process.[9] The criticism of Kenneth King from 2000, and his following prediction, remains valid:

> 'The agencies have not started with the dramatic knowledge deficits, nor with the key question of how knowledge management could assist knowledge development in the South. A continuation along their present trajectory will arguably be counter-productive; it will make agencies more certain of what they themselves have learnt, and more enthusiastic that others should share these insights, once they have been systematized.'[10]

The power dimension of knowledge and learning plays an important role in the development sector's inability to address these concerns. Many organisations are more concerned with addressing their own needs rather than those of their Southern partner organisations or intended beneficiaries. They are able to continue with this approach because the inherent and structural inequality of the relationship between donors and recipients. In addition to this, greater value is placed on Northern knowledge with little understanding of the value of multiple knowledges and multiple realities.

NGDOs and learning

It is difficult to make any absolute statements on the state of affairs with regard to the learning capacity of Northern and Southern civil society organisations'[11], but in general terms it should be acknowledged that — on account of a number of internal and external factors — the interest of the NGDO sector in concepts such as 'the learning organisation' has increased substantially over the last one and a half – two decades. There is, however, still a substantial gap between rhetoric and reality.

On the one hand, the importance of learning with regard to strengthening civil society and civil society organisations has been acknowledged by the Dutch government. For example in the White Paper 'Civil Society and Structural Poverty Reduction: Actors in Dutch civil society'[12]:

> 'But social development is a complex, non-linear process, and it is often difficult to ascertain what constitutes a positive result. ... Hence, assessing the payoff in terms of results may put disproportionate emphasis on outcomes that can be measured or verified. The problem is not what is included, but what is excluded. Looking solely at results also deters people from taking risks in situations where innovation — which inevitably entails an element of risk — would be desirable or even essential. The point is not that there may be no mistakes or that interventions must not fail, but that lessons are learnt from those mistakes. In future, CSOs will not be judged by their results alone: the quality of their monitoring and evaluation systems and *their ability to learn* [our emphasis] will also be taken into account.'[13]

On the other hand, many policies, instruments and procedures of the Dutch government *vis-à-vis* Dutch civil society organisations do not sufficiently take into account that development processes are indeed complex, non-linear processes. In turn, the NGDOs are struggling and 'major challenges of knowledge and learning in the development sector still need to be addressed'.[14]

As well as being stimulated by prescribed policies, procedures and instruments, organisations have a responsibility to effectively learn from experience. However, there has to be some awareness that information systems and reports are not the 'end products' of learning. Learning is not a technical issue, nor can it be done through providing a few trainings. It has to be a mindset, a way of doing things. Questioning, reflecting and reinventing should be elements of the daily work.

As simple as this may sound, Ramalingam argues that continuing difficulties appear to be the common prioritisation of internal, headquarters-oriented approaches which distract from the realities on the ground in the South, and that knowledge and learning work is often marginalised:

> 'The typical response to the difficulty of reorganising core processes along knowledge and learning lines has led to the widespread conceptualisation of knowledge and learning initiatives which supposedly drive organisational change, as a support function.'[15]

A further problem, also highlighted by Ramalingam, is the emphasis on best practices:

> 'The assumption that ideas can be transferred as 'best practice' from one place to another has driven much organisational learning. Rather than scanning globally and *reinventing* locally, most learning initiatives in the development sector have tried to scan globally and *apply* locally. This 'pipeline' approach to learning seriously underestimates the complexity of aid work. Therefore, best practice needs to be replaced with good principles that can provide the context for local reinvention.'[16]

Policy and operational choices of development actors in the Netherlands

If the NGDOs and the Dutch Ministry of Foreign Affairs are serious about the learning agenda, there are a number of concrete steps that will support its adoption. These relate to the subsidy framework, the nature of the learning organisation, and the issue of leadership.

The subsidy framework needs to be based on the realisation that a plan is not a blueprint that has to be implemented down to the smallest level — otherwise the building might fall down. In development, a good plan is basically an expression of a public declaration of a purpose around which people gather and not a timetable of the railways against which to check whether the project or programme is running on time. The mission and objectives are crucial but the actual trajectory and the journey will need to be flexible: 'we make the road by walking'. Here the concepts of *volition* and *agility* are of key importance:

> 'The concept of volition emphasises sense-making on the one hand (creating comprehension and purpose) and, on the other, commitment to stick to decisions that have been made. It also entails fluidity: an informed and thoughtful volition, strictly speaking, is never in error; it is, however, always subject to challenge or reformulation'.[17]

On the basis of extensive empirical research Pedler *et al.* have identified eleven characteristics of a learning organisation.[18] During the last one and a half decades in various participatory self-assessment workshops, client organisations of Context, international cooperation have been asked to identify organisational factors which facilitate and hinder learning. During these exercises most the characteristics of Pedler *et al.* have been reconfirmed. However, based on this input from the development practice a few additions need to be made: learning always takes place within the overall vision, mission and strategy of the organisation. Another important characteristic of a learning organisation is a clear mission statement, which is translated into a coherent strategy, organisational set-up and programme, and is understood and shared by all within the organisation. Furthermore, the crucial factor with regard to organisational learning is the 'organisational culture' and all tacit aspects of organisations (the invisible, the unofficial, the 'hidden connections' as Capra[19] call these issues).

When organisations are seen as 'living organisms'[20], however, organisational learning cannot be treated alike. Nancy Dixon, a leading consultant on organisational learning in the USA, argues that learning is in essence a social process.[21] Learning is thus conversation-based rather than written-based.[22] Organisational systems need to facilitate such learning through social interaction. True organisational learning involves a high degree of trust and sharing of information. It is, therefore, disconnected from activities that focus primarily on results.

In essence organisational learning is about knowledge creation and reuse and can be seen as a circular process of sharing of lessons between knowers and re-users over time. Learning is basically about knowledge creation by 'knowers' — the ones who have learnt something and are willing to share — and possible reuse by 'learners' — the ones asking the knowers and who are willing to learn and subsequently create their own story and lessons learnt. Dixon continues that the work processes within an organisation define to a certain level the type of learning and how to learn from each other. Organisational learning is basically about learning how to start the learning process on the basis of the initial questions of the learners; and about how to anticipate new sets of questions along the way.

When organisations are seen as living entities the continuous interplay between the informal dimensions and their formal manifestations is being acknowledged and reckoned with. Learning and adaptation comes from within, knowledge is embodied in the people within the system and the aliveness of the organisation resides in its informal communities of practice. The emphasis is more on tacit than on explicit knowledge. The most effective way to assess and enhance an organisation's learning potential is to support and strengthen its community of practice.

In order to make the process of organisational learning meaningful various stakeholders need to be involved right from the start, on the basis of their own commitment, terms and conditions. It is necessary to get their active participation and to provide an environment in which their creativity and organisational learning can flourish.[23] Within this context, leadership is of key importance.

Peter Senge has rightly argued that the task of leaders is to build learning organisations in which people can grow. He argues that leaders have a special role as designers and teachers and should take the lead with regard to the emergence of a collective picture of the future and the discipline of team learning. Such a leadership role is of utmost importance as many staff members of development agencies have often a rather mechanistic vision of organisations. In metaphorical terms many view organisations in the traditional Frederick Taylor kind of manner as a 'machine' instead of a 'living organism'.[24] At an operational level, this has far reaching consequences. Within such an approach the emphasis is on formal structures, systems and procedures, et cetera, and change and organisational learning is seen as something that can be engineered from outside an organisation as per Taylor's principles of 'scientific management'.[25]

But within the living organism, leadership and management are two different issues and organisational functions. By disorganising, by placing the leadership function next to the management one, the visionary element, necessary to guide the future of the organisation, would receive greater emphasis and provide an environment in which knowledge, learning and change become central. Therefore, a true leader can be recognised through the guidance she or he provides, by taking responsibilities for the choices she or he makes and her or his level of accessibility within the organisation and her partners.

Conclusions

> 'Experts, especially those dealing with local issues from afar, can, and often do, get things seriously wrong. They have a tendency to misdiagnose problems, they regularly misinterpret

what those affected actually want, and, most importantly, they frequently jump to the wrong conclusion as to what needs to be done to rectify the situation.'[26]

In summary, it can be concluded that the ability to learn from practice is in essence linked to the ability to acknowledge that development is quite often a rather complex, chaotic process, with often complex power dynamics, whereby a plan basically is an expression of an intention around which people rally and it is important to create space for acknowledging success and failure in a setting of trust-based relationships.

Despite the rhetoric, and the fact that the importance of learning is accepted in development discourse, it often appears to be a case of one step forward and one step backward, as demonstrated by international and Dutch national trends.

How can the governments encourage development organisations to make learning more central to their work? Firstly, by creating a subsidy framework that truly places learning at the centre of the development process.

How can organisations themselves make learning more central to their work? First of all, by appointing leaders who are not necessarily the managers of the organisation because these are different organisational functions which require different qualities. Leaders with a vision of development and who are manifest learners will do much to change the orientation of their organisations. Secondly, learning should not be seen organisationally as a support process: it should be at the centre of all the organisations activities. At the same time, Non-Governmental Development Organisations should ask themselves serious questions about how they learn and how they address the multiple knowledge from which they are learning. In operational terms of internal procedures that will make the learning agenda more central to the organisation and this could lead to staff assessments which include clear learning and knowledge targets, for both senior and junior staff, to promote positive attitudes and behaviour to learning and knowledge sharing of internal procedures and to build in 'reality checks' — immersion of Northern staff in Southern realities — also appears to yield benefits.

REFERENCES

1. This chapter has originally been written in 2008 at the request of Mr. Sjoerd Zanen (MDF, Ede, the Netherlands) as a short input for the policy consultation, that was taking place within the Netherlands, which was facilitated by staff members of MDF and organised by the Dutch Ministry of Foreign Affairs.
2. Senge, 1990.
3. Fowler, 1995: 143-145; Fowler, 2000.
4. Smillie & Helmich, 1993: 18.
5. Fowler, 1995: 143-156.
6. Chambers, 1997: 194.
7. Snowden at http://cognitive-edge.com/library/more/video/introduction-to-the-cynefin-framework/. Ref the Cynefin framework which has been explained in Chapter I.
8. Rihani, 2002: 235.
9. Engel, Carlsson, & van Zee, 2003.
10. King 2000, as cited in Kalseth & Cummings, 2001.
11. As stated in the letter of MDF, regarding this question dated May 30, 2008.
12. This paper was accepted by the Dutch parliament in September 2001.
13. Netherlands Ministry of Foreign Affairs, 2001: 7.
14. Ramalingam, 2005, as cited in Powell, 2006: 12.
15. Ramalingam, 2005: 30.
16. Ramalingam, 2008 in: Capacity.org.
17. Engel, 1997: 107.
18. Pedler *et al.*, 1998: Chapter 4; Senge, 1992: 22-30.
19. Capra, 2002.
20. Ref. Chapter I where, in the section on 'Different views on organisations' the notion of organisations as living organisms is elaborated.
21. Dixon, 1999.
22. Organisational learning should in other words be connected to the development of relationships, reflective conversations, probing questions and in-depth interactions.
23. Capra, 2002: 99.
24. The metaphor is borrowed from Peter Senge (1990).
25. Braverman, 1974: 85.
26. Rihani, 2002: 233.

Chapter IV

Ten Dilemmas Concerning Capacity Development

Fons van der Velden and *Udan Fernando*[1]

Introduction

In the preceding chapters a foundation has been provided with regard to the state of affairs in capacity development (Chapter I); a case study has been presented with a practical and recent example of facilitating a capacity development process with a Non-Governmental Development Organisation in North India (Chapter II); and reflections about the relationship between the Dutch government and civil society organisations in the Netherlands were provided in Chapter III. In the present and concluding chapter of this book ten major dilemmas concerning capacity development are presented. Some of these dilemmas relate to paradigm issues (1–3), other dilemmas relate specifically to the core purpose of capacity development (4– 5), the methodology (6–9) and the future (10).

1. What is capacity development?

Chapter I already highlighted the fact that different perspectives can be distinguished in relation to the origin and meaning of the term capacity development (CD) and that these should not be seen as mutually exclusive alternatives.[2]

As described in Chapter I, the first and predominant perspective in the literature is that CD is 'a technical solution to a technical problem'. The important question here is: 'how can policy and practice contribute effectively to development goals?' and hence within such an approach the emphasis is on aid effectiveness (*ref.* Paris Agenda, Accra Declaration et cetera). Growing concern about aid effectiveness since the late 1990s has produced extensive policy literature on how capacity development should be supported.[3] In essence this perspective takes an instrumentalist approach and considers capacity development as a means to achieve a larger goal, in this case aid effectiveness.

A second school of thought sees the concept as a way to achieve social justice. From this perspective, capacity development is an end in itself, closely related to emancipatory development. Morgan defines capacity as: 'Capacity is about *empowerment and identity*, properties that allow an organisation or system to survive, to grow, diversify and become more complex'.[4] Within this context, Clark and Oswald argue that capacity development should be understood as 'a collective process of learning in action for social change. Support for capacity development processes demands a critical development practice that implies mutual learning, with an emphasis on reflective and experiential approaches'.[5]

In line with Kaplan's definition, capacity development can thus be defined as '. . . . . the increased ability and power to do something in particular (functional capacity), or increase resilience and autonomy (intrinsic capacity)'.[6] This definition conveys the notion of a change process — there is no conscious intervention regarding capacity development; no 'agency' either internal or external.[7] Capacity building refers to support to capacity development, to capacity enhancement. 'It is a purposeful, conscious effort to bring about capacity development.'[8] In this context it is important to note that 'building' does not imply starting from scratch. 'Capacity building' suggests a purpose to the activities, whereas 'capacity development' may be viewed as a broader term, which can cover a process with no involvement of 'agency' i.e. no purposeful intervention.[9]

Capacity relates to competencies — energies, skills and

abilities of individuals. Capabilities relate to a collective ability of a group or a system to do something. Tacit aspects of capacity such as experience, intuition and institutional memory are aspects that cannot be documented.

Other authors and practitioners, such as Kühl, distance themselves from the term CD and they criticise its 'self serving use' by development actors. The argument is that the term CD is used as an attempt to legitimise — in high and medium inccme countries — the activities of development organisations, and does not qualify as evidence that CD actually works in low and medium income countries. In Kühl's view northern organisations, faced with a crisis in moral authority and legitimacy, engage in conceptual novelty. Kühl argues that CD can be viewed as 'a political technology of neoliberal governance' constructing 'compliant communities' taking responsibility for their own future.[10]

The foregoing sections show that CD carries many definitions, ranging from a narrow, technical and instrumentalist approach to a broad, qualitative and intrinsic approach. CD is not an apolitical phenomenon. How capacity is defined and who is defining it determines the politics of CD. Hence, CD runs the risk of being stretched to serve one's interests.

2. Capacity development for whom: single actor *versus* multi-actor systems

If organisations are to be understood as open systems[11] or as living organisms with numerous hidden connections inside and outside the system, capacity development cannot be understood as an isolated phenomenon. It is intrinsically linked with the 'other' or many 'others'. As such, CD is interlinked in terms of actors, capabilities and processes and, therefore, an indivisible process. One actor needs the other to change its capacity and *vice versa*. The capability of one cannot be developed without a corresponding change or compatibility in the other. Within the development sector a mere provision of 'inputs' alone — in the form of financial resources or advice — from a donor cannot develop the capacity of the Southern partner organisation. The donor's own policy, staffing and relational attributes should be compatible with the change that is desired in the Southern partner organisation. This requires a mutuality and reciprocity in CD. As such, the process of CD does not take place only in the domain of the Southern partner organisations but also in that of the donor.

Moreover, it is often assumed that CD starts from within individuals and organisations and then permeates into society. Recent research shows that '. . . . . working with multiple actors could be an effective form of CD in its own right. When well done, multi-actor engagement builds the combined as well as the individual and organisational capacities of actors within the system, and enhances the quality of the policies and regulations that influence their interrelationships'.[12] It is important to recognise that capacity and capacity development is highly relational and that '. . . . . many forms of effective capacity grow in the interactive spaces between actors'.[13]

Summing up, the capacity of 'them' is also the capacity of 'us'. Hence, the indivisibility of CD emerges as a major lesson. A main implication of this lesson is the blurring of the demarcation between endogenous and exogenous processes of CD.[14]

3. Images of organisations

In the literature about this subject and amongst development practitioners there are many different perspectives and frameworks with regard to organisations and capacity development. In Chapter I, a schematic overview has been given in terms of metaphors and images of organisations varying from the traditional Taylor image of an organisation, to the INTRAC model which pays attention to 'positioning', 'being', 'doing' and 'relating', the 5C model and the notion that organisations are living entities.[15] The differences between what may be called the conventional and the new science view of organisations can be summarised as follows (refer Table 4.1).

Table 4.1: Views of organisations

New science view	*Conventional view*
1. Company is defined by its ideas, business processes, relationships, and interfaces with partners.	Company is defined by its products, people, technology and hierarchical structure.
2. The future into which the organisation lives is the source of change.	The past from which the organisation came is the source of change.
3. Change is probabilistic and non-linear and tends toward uncertain outcomes.	Change is regular, predictable, and tends toward stable points.
4. Company or division has irreducible qualities.	Company is the sum of its value-added activities.
5. Organisation can be influenced but not controlled.	Organisation is defined and controlled by senior managers.
6. Company is broadly integrated with its environment; everything is interconnected. Boundaries are fluid.	Boundaries separate people, activities and units.
Values	
7. Relationships require trust.	Relationships require control.
8. Many viewpoints, consideration of a variety of possibilities.	Singe viewpoint, one best way.
9. Sharing, win/win, listening, dialogue.	Right/wrong, win/lose, proving a point.

Source: Laszlo & Laugel, 2000 : 30.

The perceptions people have about organisations need to be seen as a continuum and not as a stringent model (as in '*All models are wrong, some models are useful*' — George Box). However, these perceptions do have far reaching implications for the formulation of capacity development policies, instruments and procedures. In other words, the different theories of change engender different CD strategies. The 'machine' image paves the way for external CD strategies with a great deal of emphasis on the formal characteristics of an organisation; change is something that can be engineered from outside an organisation as per Taylor's principles of 'scientific management'.[16] The 'living organism' image stimulates CD approaches that strive to capture the dynamic and complex context in which the organisation is embedded and that requires constant change to adapt. The capabilities that need to be developed go beyond the 'formal' components, i.e., address the tacit and complex aspects of organisations.

In terms of change processes the difference may be summarised as follows (Table 4.2).

Table 4.2: Classic *versus* new organisational development

	Classic OD usually includes	*New OD may include*
1.	Influence from classic science and modern thought and philosophy	Influence from the new sciences and post-modern thought and philosophy
2.	Reality is an objective fact	Reality is socially constructed
3.	There is a single reality	There are multiple realities
4.	Truth is transcendent and discoverable	Trust is immanent and emerges from the situation
5.	Reality can be discovered using rational and analytic processes	Reality is negotiated and may involve power and political processes
6.	Collecting and applying valid data using objective problem-solving methods leads to change	Creating new social agreements through explicit or implicit negotiation leads to change
7.	Change can be created, planned and managed	Change is inherent and can be self-organising
8.	Change is episodic and linear	Change is continuous and/or cyclical
9.	Emphasis on changing behaviour and what one does	Emphasis on changing mindsets and how one thinks

Source: Marshak, 2005.

4. Capacity for what purpose?

In line with the earlier highlighted debate about 'What is capacity development?' The question arises: 'Capacity for what purpose?'. Both at policy and operational level there are three major choices to be made.

Intrinsic or instrumental capacity development[17]

Most of the definitions of capacity, such as the UNDP definition[18] ('The ability of individuals, institutions and societies to perform functions, solve problems and set and achieve objectives in a sustainable manner') and the OECD/DAC definition ('The ability of people, organisations and society as a whole to manage their affairs successfully')[19] associate the term capacity with action, i.e., the ability or the power to do, to perform. This is a rather instrumental definition of capacity development. Others find such performance-related definitions too narrow and emphasise the intrinsic or robust capacity of an organisation; the ability or power within, i.e., to be or to exist. The definitions of Peter Morgan[20] and Allan Kaplan ('..... the ability of an organisation to function as a resilient, strategic and autonomous entity ..... [which is] capable of sovereign focus and direction, to changing circumstances, and of acting decisively to impact on, and change'[21]) fit into this category. This is not merely a semantic issue as the intrinsic and instrumental approaches serve different purposes and lead to a different intervention repertoire.

Types of change

As has already been argued in Chapter I[22] it is important to define what type of change is being pursued. Basically, three archetypes of organisational change can be distinguished: developmental change, transitional change and transformational change. [23]

Developmental change represents the improvement of an existing situation. The key focus is strengthening or correcting what already exists in an organisation, thus ensuring improved performance, continuity and greater satisfaction. Transitional change is more complex. It is the required response to more significant shifts in environmental forces or marketplace requirements for success. Rather than simply improving 'what is', transitional change replaces 'what is' with something entirely different. In transformational change, human and cultural issues are normally the key drivers. Transformational change is the radical shift from one state of being to another, so significant that it needs a shift of culture, behaviour and mindset to be implemented successfully and in a sustained manner over time.[24]

The first two change processes are characterised by a process with some degree of control and order, while transformational change is normally a much more chaotic affair and cannot be controlled.

Dimensions of an organisation

Capacities can be divided into 'hard' and 'soft'. 'Hard' refers for example to the capacity to build infrastructure and manage finances; and 'soft' refers to, for example, the capacity to manage knowledge, communication, trust building, networking, 'making sense of messy social situations', et cetera.[25]

Kaplan divides soft capacities into tangible and intangible. The former refers to visible systems and processes; the latter refers to less obvious capacities such as the capability to relate. Clark and Oswald argue that: 'Whilst hard and soft, as well as tangible and intangible, capacities are all important, it is the soft and intangible capacities that are more difficult to identify and develop, but, ... are crucial in supporting emancipatory social change'.[26]

The 'capacity for what purpose' relates to the kind of change envisaged and the place where the change takes place. One CD process may be a merely instrumental one to 'perform' or 'deliver' whereas another can be an intrinsic one that involves a qualitative change within an organisation. The type of change can also vary qualitatively and quantitatively while the change can relate to material aspects of an organisation as well as to 'soft' aspects. These three dimensions suggest that the type of change determines the nature and scope of CD. This means that a CD process will have different scopes, depths and sites of change.

5. Where do we pitch capacity development?

Among development practitioners in capacity development programmes the emphasis historically has been on Human Resources Development (HRD), Organisational Development

(OD) and /or Institutional Development (ID).[27] Of late a realisation has emerged that CD should be comprehensive and henceforth requires efforts at different levels.

At the one end of the spectrum we have the realisation that CD first and foremost concerns 'people'. Individuals are the key; their behaviour, confidence and trust: 'Development starts with self'.[28] Issues of (personal) leadership are crucial in the context of transitional and transformational change. At the same time there is the realisation that complex multi-faceted problems of poverty, marginalisation and violation of human rights require complex multi-actor responses in order to contribute to sustainable solutions.

While engaging in CD, strategic decisions need to be made regarding where to 'pitch' a contribution in the continuum reaching from capacity as a deeply personal issue to an issue of systems-wide, systemic change. This means that 'pitching' can start with an immediate need for CD, say staff development, but at the same time, that capability should be embedded in the larger organisational and institutional setting as they are interlinked. The challenge lies in understanding where the initial CD effort should be 'pitched' and then identify the other inter-linkages at different levels.

6. Who's driving?

In the literature about organisational change there is a consensus that genuine, authentic organisational change comes from within (endogenous). Ideally speaking organisations perform a self-assessment at the beginning of change processes, design their own change plan, including definition of priorities and measurable objectives, contract external support (if any) and finance such a change process from internal sources. As argued elsewhere such a line of reasoning may be seen as a 'politically correct position', but reality is far more complex as such an approach requires a high degree of organisational self awareness and a minimum standard of organisational capabilities.[29]

On the basis of recent research[30], it can be noted that external factors, donor policies, external opportunities, interventions and actors often play a considerable role in the emergence, facilitation and implementation of the CD process.[31] CD has often emerged on account of external stimuli, and less often on account of internal learning loops. A recent insight is, therefore, that the value and importance of an external stimulus is explicitly mentioned and that an externally initiated (exogenous) approach to CD may have a value in itself. As long as there are systems and procedures in place to enhance the local ownership and commitment, an internally initiated, led and located CD is not necessarily the more desirable or feasible option. Partnership between capacity development service providers and a client organisation with regard to CD can bring about substantial benefits based on comparative advantages.

Another lesson with regard to the endogenous-exogenous divide is that CD processes which may at the beginning of a CD process be characterised as exogenous can develop towards the endogenous end of the spectrum in terms of ownership, linking to internal learning processes, etc. In this sense the notion of CD as an exclusively endogenous process needs to be demystified. Moreover, the categories endogenous-exogenous should be seen as two ends of a wide spectrum: positions are not black and white — there is a wide range of greys in between.[32] In the change practice it is important to read situations and act accordingly and to avoid rather rigid 'one size fits all' approaches.

7. Process versus 'spark'

Capacity development is often understood as a process. Four dimensions of a CD process can be identified[33]:

1. *Content*: One should know the market.
2. *Process*: One should know how to organise.
3. *People*: One should understand their behaviour, joy, frustration, etc.
4. *Benefits*: Keep an eye on results.

When monitoring CD processes, these four dimensions should be taken into account. These four dimensions are interrelated and should be kept in balance. This does not mean that equal attention should be paid to the four dimensions at all times. Certain dimensions need more attention than others at different stages of a CD process.

Though the 'process' thinking on CD is still relevant and valid, it should not be understood as a hard and fast rule. In other words CD does not always have to be a process; sometimes a 'spark' can lead to change. Recent action research includes evidence of some case studies in which such 'sparks' played a significant role in the CD effort.[34] Therefore, it is recommended to be careful with standardisation. The challenge of handling 'sparks' is that they cannot be predicted or planned and therefore cannot be monitored in a pre-designed manner. This does not mean that a CD effort should entirely depend on 'sparks'. Rather, they are a 'bonus' when they occur.

8. What can relative outsiders do?

The CD strategies and the intervention roles of the actors are influenced by the context of the organisation, the core purpose of the organisation, stage of organisational evolution, types of change being targeted, et cetera. In Chapter I it has been stated that there are in principle a number of different roles that outsiders can play in fostering organisational change, such as consultant or advisor.[35] The success of change processes depends greatly on advisors playing an appropriate role at an appropriate time.[36] Consulting roles can be described along a directive and non-directive continuum. Three archetypes of roles may be distinguished: expert, advisor, facilitator.[37] In addition to the directive and non-directive continuum one more position may be added: self-organising.

It should be noted that there is no single best way to support, facilitate, or encourage change within organisations. Adequate scanning of the environment, mapping of stakeholders and 'reading' the existing situation are, therefore, important conditions to enable the appropriate choice of CD. Choices concerning the type of change that is required need to be made in accordance with the specific situation, the type of organisation and the relationship between the organisation and the outside party.

Furthermore, on the basis of recent research the question has emerged as to what the extent of the contribution of relative outsiders can be. Phlix, in the study about the association PSO, seems to suggest that relative outsiders can only contribute to single loop learning ('are we doing things right?'). Double loop learning ('are we doing the right things?') or triple loop learning ('is our work based on the correct assumptions?') are not likely to be achieved through the contribution of relative outsiders.[38] The outsiders' role is not ruled out, however, they can certainly play a role in the CD process. But it should be played carefully and thoughtfully, and in an appropriate manner to avoid the CD process being excessively driven by outsiders as that may undermine local ownership.

9. How to measure capacity development?

The subject of how to measure the results of capacity development efforts relates to some of the paradigm issues which have been discussed in the foregoing dilemmas: is development seen as a linear process or positioned within a complexity perspective?

Baser & Morgan (ECDPM study report) state:

> 'It is usually assumed that there exists a fairly direct line of causation between improved capacity and better results. This basic pattern of thinking has been reinforced by the 'inputs–outputs–outcomes–impact' framework that creates a sense of linear progression and escalating importance as the focus moves from left to right. The more capacity, the better the performance, the more results. The findings of the case research have led us to rethink this view'.[39]

These observations lead among others to the question whether evaluation of capacity development programmes needs to use an intervention-result-chain focus ('theory' or 'policy based') or whether a more evidence based approach ('what has emerged') is more appropriate.

The second major debate in this subject area centres on the issue of how outcomes of capacity development can be assessed. Ubels and Fowler state:

> 'A first type of development results is improved capacity itself. Capacity building was a crucial developmental goal in its own right that entailed equipping a country, a region, an organisation or an individual with attitudes, values, behaviours that they needed to make progress.'[40]

Others, such as the Policy and Operations Department of the Dutch Ministry of Foreign Affairs (IOB) seem to follow Peter Drucker's adagio 'there is nothing inside organisations, only costs' and henceforth results can only be measured in terms of outputs, i.e., outcomes at the programme ('doing') level. Improved capacity from this perspective is an organisation implementing project and/or programmes as per a certain standard; capacity is seen as an 'input' or as a 'means' to achieve higher-order programme development results.[41] The ECDPM study by Baser and Morgan '. . . . . has highlighted the limitations of relying exclusively on a narrow, instrumental way of improving capability for generating development results'.[42]

Within this context it should be noted that external pressures, particularly from funding environments, push organisations to differentiate CD efforts that can be measured in terms of results. From this tendency there emerges a trend of support to instrumental CD strategies. Such short-term and isolated CD activities may erode the potential of structural/ political change, which requires a long-term and embedded/ comprehensive approach. Such an approach also contradicts basic premises of CD which understand organisations as open complex systems and CD as an endogenous, non-linear process.

The 5C model's stress on 'coherence', in this sense, raises concern regarding the organisation's predicament of being torn between the divides of 'instrumentalist' and 'intrinsic' CD.

10. Gap between rhetoric and reality: the need for appropriate practice

Many authors argue that the ins and outs of CD are complex and difficult to comprehend. Gosses, in a publication of the Dutch Ministry of Foreign Affairs, writes of 'The mystery of capacity development'. James and Wrigley embark upon an 'Investigating the Mystery of Capacity Building'; Morgan speaks of 'a risky, murky, messy business with unpredictable, unqualifiable outcomes'.[43]

The mystery of CD needs to be demystified. Over the last decade considerable progress has been made in defining capacity development. A number of relevant studies from different sources indicate important emerging areas of conceptual congruence. A whole body of literature has emerged that provides rather deep insights into the ins and outs of CD. In Chapter I an overview has been provided about the 'sins' and 'virtues' that have been distilled by James from a survey of the relevant literature.[44] Lipson and Hunt have made a similar overview (see Box 4.1).[45]

In Chapter I, an analysis has been presented showing why it is apparently so difficult to apply lessons learnt.[46] Northern donors continue to set the agenda for capacity building; contents of capacity development often reflect donor priorities; power relations have a profound influence on capacity development and a two-way process of learning and change is often missing. Moreover, support of International NGDOs for development of local capacity development providers is often missing and appears to be more instrumental than strategic; in terms of methods, emphasis is still on training and technical assistance[47] and '. . . . . over-reliance on [these] structured, even formulaic, approaches to capacity development suggests that

Box 4.1: Good practices with regard to capacity development

1. **Context**
   - Analysis
   - Cultural understanding
   - Relationship mapping
   - Supply profile
2. **Agenda**
   - Explore and articulate
   - Clarity on the 'for what?' question
   - Sensitivity on personal interests
3. **Knowledge Base**
   - Develop conceptual frameworks
   - Ensure consistency of language/terms
   - Invest in learning
   - Ensure reflective practice
   - Engage in debate
4. **Approach**
   - Ensure 'ownership'
   - Appropriate interventions (one-size does not fit all)
   - Acknowledge existing capacities
   - Systemic/holistic
   - Empower (to choose service providers; to influence design, timing, etc.)
   - Ensure accountability
   - Clarity of roles
   - Recognition of power dynamics
   - Build trust
   - Recognise yourself as part of the process

many agencies are avoiding facing up to some of the messy and complex human dimensions of capacity development'.[48] Moreover, many international NGDOs lack a strategic approach to capacity development.[49] The performance with regard to resourcing is mixed as well as the monitoring and evaluation of capacity development experiences.[50]

In view of the above, it should be concluded that the emphasis should no longer be on distilling good practices with regard to CD, but on applying the lessons that have been learnt, as the gap between rhetoric and reality is often too big. This requires a shift from conceptual to practical issues: what are organisational and institutional facts that hinder and facilitate 'good' capacity development? In such an analysis issues may be grouped per sphere of control, influence and concern.

REFERENCES

1. At the time that this contribution was written (2011) Udan Fernando worked as a senior consultant at Context, international cooperation, Utrecht, the Netherlands. The research from which this chapter emerged was mainly funded by Partos (Amsterdam, the Netherlands) (Van der Velden and Fernando, 2011). The work within the Hivos curriculum (The Hague, the Netherlands) has helped considerably in presenting some of our major observations in a succinct manner. Earlier research that was funded by among others SNV (Van der Velden *et al.*, 2005) and EED (Bonn Germany) (Van der Velden *et al.* 2008).
2. Clark and Oswald, 2010: 3–4.
3. Refer publications from the UNDP (2008, 2009, 2010), EU and the OECD.
4. Morgan, 2006: p. x.
5. Clark and Oswald, 2010: 3.
6. Lipson and Hunt, 2008: 31. (It related to Kolb's experiential learning cycle of reflecting; connecting; testing; doing.)
7. Lipson personal communication, January 11, 2010.
8. *Ibid.*
9. Lipson and Hunt, 2008: 31.
10. Kühl, 2009: 575.
11. Refer Chapter I where the 5C Model developed by ECDPM has been described.
12. Acquaye-Badoo *et al.*, 2010: 4.
13. *Ibid.*, p. 6.
14. See for a further elaboration of this argument dilemma 6.
15. Refer Chapter I.
16. Braverman, 1974: 85.
17. Refer Chapter 1, paragraph 3.
18. UNDP, 2006.
19. DAC, 2006.
20. Morgan, 2006.
21. Kaplan, 1999 (cited in Lipson and Hunt, 2008: 11).
22. Paragraph 4.
23. See among others: Aldrich, 1999; Ardon *et al.*, 2005; De Caluwé & Vermaak, 2002; Thaw, 2002.
24. Anderson and Ackerman Anderson, 2001: 39.
25. Woodhill, 2010: 47; Clark and Oswald, 2010: 5.
26. Clark and Oswald, 2010: 5.
27. Refer Van der Velden and Leenknegt, 2006 and Chapter 1 (paragraph 3) and Chapter II of the present volume.

28. Chigudu, 2010.
29. Hoebink and Van der Velden, 2002.
30. Van der Velden and Fernando, 2011: 83–84.
31. This has as well happened in the case of Cecoedecon, refer the case study in Chapter II. External support includes services such as facilitating reflection through dialogue, agenda setting, technical contributions in combination with local demands and initiatives and local expertise and existing local knowledge.
32. Baser and Morgan argue: 'Few endogenous efforts at capacity development anywhere in the world are completely autonomous and self-contained. Most are influenceα to some degree by external ideas and pressures' (Baser and Morgan, 2008: 9). External impulses do not necessarily have to come from donors but can as well emerge from communities, sister organisations.
33. Van der Velden and Leenknegt, 2006.
34. Van der Velden and Fernando, 2011.
35. The first part of the paragraph is borrowed from Van der Velden, Leenknegt and Haijtink, 2005.
36. James, 1998: 32.
37. See Chapter 1, paragraph 5.
38. Phlix, 2010.
39. Baser and Morgan, 2008: 86.
40. Ubels and Acquaye-Baddoo, Fowler, 2010: 19.
41. *Ibid.*
42. *Ibid.*
43. Gosses, 2007: 113; James and Wrigley, 2007; Morgan, 1997.
44. James, 2010: 19–21.
45. Lipton and Hunt, 2008.
46. See Chapter 1, paragraph 7.
47. Lipson and Warren, 2006.
48. James, 2010: 15.
49. Lipson and Warren, 2006; James, 2010.
50. A few attempts are being made to develop approaches for monitoring and evaluation, these include Roche, 1999 (Chapter 7), Bakewell, 2003 (Chapter 10) and Engel *et al.*, 2007.

Bibliography

Acquaye-Baddoo, N., Brouwers, J., *et al.* (2010) Multi-actor systems as entry points to capacity development. *Capacity.Org*, *41*, 4-7.

Aldrich, H. (1999) *Organisations Evolving*. London: Sage Publications.

Anderson, D. & Ackerman Anderson, L. (2001) *Beyond Change Management. Advanced Strategies for Today's Transformational Leaders*. San Francisco: Jossey-Bass/Pfeiffer.

Ardon, A., & Bertels, R. (eds.) (2005) *Duurzaam Veranderen*. (Sustainable change.) Amsterdam: Holland Consulting Group.

Bakewell, O.; Pratt B.; and Adams J. (2003) *Sharpening the Development Process: A Practical Guide to Monitoring and Evaluation*. Oxford: INTRAC.

Bartczak, L. (Ed.) (2005) *A Funder's Guide to Organisational Assessment: Tools, Processes, and Their Use in Building Capacity*. Saint Paul, MN: Fieldstone Alliance.

Baser, H., & Morgan, P. (2008) *Capacity, Change and Performance. Study Report*. Discussion Paper No. 59B. Maastricht: ECDPM.

Berg, E. J. (1993) *Rethinking Technical Cooperation. Reforms for Capacity Building in Africa*. New York: UNDP.

Bieckmann, F. (2008) Deep Democracy – Reinventing citizen action, Civic Driven Change Initiative. *The Broker*, *10*, 9-16.

Bolger, J. (2000) Capacity Development: Why, What and How. *Capacity Development Occasional Series, 1(1)*.

Braverman, H. (1974) *Labour and Monopoly Capital: The Degradation of Work in the Twentieth Century*. New York: Monthly Review Press.

Brouwers, J. *et al.* (2010) *Social Return on Investment. A Practical Guide for the Development Cooperation Sector*. Utrecht: Context, International Cooperation.

Browne, S. (2002) *Developing Capacity Through Technical Cooperation; Country Experiences*. London/New York: Earthscan/UNDP.

Capra, F. (2005) *The Hidden Connections. A Science for Sustainable Living*. London: Harper Collins Publishers.

Chambers, R. (1997) *Whose Reality Counts?* London: Intermediate Technology Publications.

Champion, D., Kiel, D., & McLendon, J. (1985) The consulting role grid. In R. Lynton and U. Pareek, *Facilitating Development: Readings for Trainers, Consultants and Policy Makers*. Thousand Oaks/London: Sage Publications (p. 124-130).

Chigudu, H. (2010) *Capacity Development Evaluation Process: Case Study Coalition of African Lesbians*. Amsterdam/Utrecht: Partos/ Context, international cooperation.

Clark, P., & Oswald, K. (2010) Introduction: Why Reflect Collectively on Capacities for Change? *IDS Bulletin, 41*, 1-12.

DAC Network on Governance (2006) *The Challenge of Capacity Development: Working Towards Good Practice*. Retrieved October 2006, from www.worldbank.org/INTCDRC/Resources/oecd_challenge_of_capacity_development.pdf

De Caluwé, L., & Vermaak, H. (2002) *Leren Veranderen. Een handboek voor de veranderkundige*. (Learning to change. A manual for the change expert.) Deventer: Kluwer.

De Geus, A. (1997) *The Living Company*. Harvard: Harvard Business School Press.

Dixon, N. (1999) *The Organizational Learning Cycle: How We can Learn Collectively*. London: Gower Publishing Company.

Eade, D. (1997) *Capacity-Building: An Approach to People-Centred Development*. Oxford: Oxfam.

ECDPM (2004) *Institutional Development: Learning by Doing and Sharing. Approaches and Tools for Supporting Institutional Development*. European Centre for Development Policy Management (ECDPM), Netherlands Ministry of Foreign Affairs, Poverty Policy and Institutional Development Division (DSA/AI), draft booklet.

——, 2008 *Policy Management brief* 21, December.

Engel, P.G.H. (1997) *The Social Organisation of Innovation: A Focus on Stakeholder Interaction*. Amsterdam: Royal Tropical Institute.

Engel, P.; Carlsson, C. & van Zee, A. (2003) *Internalising Evaluation Results through Learning: Complementary Perspectives, Dilemmas and Some Lessons Learned*. Maastricht: European Centre for Development Policy Management.

Engel, P.; Keijzer N.; Land T. (2007) *A Balanced Approach to Monitoring and Evaluating Capacity and Performance: A Proposal for a Framework*. Discussion paper No 58E, Maastricht, ECDPM.

Eyben, R. (Ed.) (2006) *Relationships for Aid*. London: Earthscan.

Fowler, A. (1995) Assessing NGO Performance: Difficulties, Dilemmas and A Way Forward. In Edwards, M. & Hulme, D., *Non-Governmental Organisations – Performance and Accountability; Beyond the Magic Bullet*. London: Earthscan.

——, 2000 *Partnerships: Negotiating Relationships: A Resource for Non-*

Gouvernmental Development Organisations. INTRAC Occasional Paper Series No. 32. Oxford: INTRAC.

Fowler, A., 2006 *Systemic Change for Promoting Local Capacity Development,* Working Paper for Stichting Nederlands Vrijwilligers (SNV). Johannesburg: Netherlands Development Organisation.

Fowler, A & Ubels, J. (2010) The multi-faceted nature of Capacity: Two Leading Frameworks. In Ubels, J., Acquaye-Baddoo, N., & Fowler, A. (Eds.), *Capacity Development in Practice.* London: Earthscan Ltd. (http://www.snvworld.org/en/Pages/CapacityDevelopment.aspx).

Frediani, A.A. (2010) Sen's Capability Approach as a Framework to the Practice of Development. *Development in Practice, 2,* 20.

Fukuda-Parr, S., Lopes, C., & Malik, K. (2002) *Capacity for Development: New Solutions to Old Problems.* London/New York: Earthscan Publications/UNDP.

Gosses, A. (2007) *Stop Teaching, Start Learning; the Mystery of Capacity Development.* The Hague: Dutch Ministry of Foreign Affairs (DEK/BA) (http://www.dochas.ie/pages/resources/documents/stopteaching-startlearning.pdf)

Gubbels, P., & Koss, C. (2000) *From the Roots Up: Strengthening Organisational Capacity Through Guided Self Assessment.* World Neighbours Field Guide 2, Capacity Building. Oklahoma City: World Neighbours.

Hivos (2009) *Hivos and Capacity Development; Preparatory Note for Programme Evaluation Capacity Development.* The Hague: Hivos.

Hoebink, P., & Van der Velden, F. (2002) *From Volunteerism to Professionalism: Technical Assistance of the Netherlands in a Change.* Paper for the 10th EADI General Conference 'EU Enlargement in a Changing World Challenges for Development Cooperation in the 21st Century', Working Group 'Aid and Development', Ljubljana.

Huyse, H.; Phlix, G.; and Dehaene, C. (2010) *Evaluation of NGO Partnerships Aimed at Capacity Development.* Leuven: HIVA.

I/C Consult (2001) *Looking at Organisations – Concept Behind Organisation Scan.* Retrieved from http://www.nl/documents/looking_at_ organisations_2aug01.doc

IOB (2011) *Facilitating Resourcefulness; Synthesis Report of the Evaluation of Dutch Support to Capacity Development.* The Hague: IOB/Dutch Ministry of Foreign Affairs.

James, R. (1998) *Demystifying Organisation Development. Practical Capacity-Building Experiences of African Ngos.* INTRAC NGO Management and Policy Series No 7. Oxford: INTRAC.

——, (2002) *People and Change. Exploring Capacity-Building in NGOs.* INTRAC NGO Management and Policy Series No. 15. Oxford: INTRAC.

——, (2010) Vices and Virtues in Capacity Development by International NGOs, *IDS Bulletin, 41 (3),* 13-23.

James, R. & Hailey J. (2007) *Capacity Building for NGOs; Making It Work*. Oxford: International NGO Training Research Centre (INTRAC).

James, R. & Wrigley, R. (2007) *Investigating the Mystery of Capacity Building: Learning from the Praxis Programme*. Praxis paper 18. Oxford: International NGO Training Research Centre (INTRAC).

Johnson, S. & Ludema, J.D. (1997) *Partnering to Build and Measure Organisational Capacity: Lessons from NGOs Around the World. Grand Rapids*. MI: Christian Reformed World Relief Committee.

Kalseth, K. & Cummings, S., A. (2001) Knowledge Management: development strategy or business strategy? In *Information Development 17 (3)*, 163–172.

Kaplan, A. (1999) *The Development of Capacity*. Woodstock: CDRA (originally published as a Development Dossier by the United Nations Non-governmental Liaison Service).

——, (2002) *Development Practitioners and Social Process. Artists of the Invisible*. London: Pluto Press.

Kruse, S.E. *et al.* (1998) *Institutional Development in Norwegian Bilateral Assistance; Development Through Institutions? Synthesis Report*. Oslo: Ministry of Foreign Affairs.

Kühl, S. (2009) Capacity Development as the Model for Development Aid Organisations. *Development and Change, 40 (3)*, 551-577.

Land, T.; Hauck, V.; and H. Baser (2009) *Capacity Change and Performance: Capacity Development: Between Planned Interventions and Emergent Processes Implications for Development Cooperation*. Policy Management Brief No. 22. Maastricht: ECDPM.

Laszlo, C., & Laugel, J.F. (2000) *Large-Scale Organizational Change: An Executive's Guide*. Boston: Butterworth-Heinemann.

Lipson, B. & Hunt, M. (2008) *Capacity Building Framework: A Value-Based Programming Guide*. Oxford: International NGO Training Research Centre (INTRAC).

Lipson, B. & Warren, H. (2006) *International Non-Governmental Organisations' Approaches to Civil Society Capacity Building: Overview Survey*. INTRAC Paper for Capacity Building Conference, Oxford. Retrieved December 16, 2009, from http://intrac.org/pages/CBProgramme.html.

Lopes, C., & T. Theison (Eds.) (2003) *Ownership, Leadership and Transformation: Can We Do Better for Capacity Development?* London/New York: Earthscan Publications/UNDP.

Lusthaus, C.; Adrien, M.H.; Anderson, G.; and Carden, F. (2000) *Enhancing Organisational Performance. A Toolbox for Self-Assessment*. New Delhi: International Development Research Centre/ Vikas Publishing House.

Marshak, R (2005) Is there new OD? *Seasonings: A Journal by Senior OD Practitioners* 1 (1) http://www.odnetwork.org/publications.

Morgan, G. (1989) *Creative Organisation Theory: A Resource Book*. London:

Sage Publications.
——, *(1997) Images of Organisation* (2nd ed.). London: Sage Publications.
Morgan, P. (1998) *Capacity and Capacity Development – Some Strategies.* Hull: Policy Branch, CIDA.
——, (2006) *The Concept of Capacity.* Maastricht: European Centre for Development Policy and Management (ECDPM).
Netherlands Ministry of Foreign Affairs (2001) *Civil Society and Structural Poverty Reduction: Actors in Dutch Civil Society*. The Hague: Ministry of Foreign Affairs.
Nussbaum, M. (2011) *Creating Capabilities: the Human Development Approach.* Cambridge: The Belknap Press of the Harvard University Press.
Patton, M.Q. (2011) *Developmental Evaluation: Applying Complexity Concepts to Enhance Innovation and Use*. New Uork: The Guilford Press.
Pedler, M., and Aspinwall, K. (1998) *A Concise Guide to the Learning Organisation. Managing Change and Learning is the No. 1 Task – Wherever You Work*. London: Lemos & Crane.
Phlix, G.; Van der Velden; F., De Wal, M.; and Zevenbergen, K. (2012) *Facilitating Organisational Learning; Insights from Practice*. The Hague: PSO.
Powell, M. (2006) Which knowledge? Whose reality? An overview of knowledge used in the development sector. *Development in Practice*, Volume 16, Issue 6, 518–532.
Ramalingam, B. (2005) Implementing Knowledge Strategies: Lessons from international development agencies, *Working Paper 244 Overseas Development Institute*. London: Overseas Development Institute.
——, (2008) Organizational learning for aid, and learning aid organisations. *Capacity.org # 33*.
Rilke, R.M. (2000) *Letters to a Young Poet*. Novato: New World Library (Original 1903).
Rihani, S. (2002) *Complex Systems Theory and Development Practice: Understanding Non-Linear Realities*. London: Zed Books.
Roche, C. (1999) *Impact Assessment for Development Agencies. Learning to Value Change*. Oxford: Oxfam.
Schein, E. (1999) *Process Consultation Revisited. Building the Helping Relationship*. Reading: Addison-Wesley Publishing.
Sen, A. (1999) *Development as Freedom* Oxford: OUP.
Senge, P. (1990) *The Fifth Discipline: The Art and Practice of the Learning Organisation.* New York: Currency Doubleday.
Smillie, I. & Helmich, H. (1993) Non-governmental organisations and governments: Stakeholders for development. Paris: OECD.
Soal, S. (2004) *Holding Infinity: Guiding Social Processes: A Workbook for*

Development Practitioners. Woodstock: CDRA (Stoner) J. A. F., Freeman, E., & Gilbert D.R.

Stoner, J.A.f.; E. Freeman and D.R. Gilbert, (1993) *Management* (6th ed.). New Jersey: Prentice-Hall.

Thaw, D. (2002) Stepping into the River of Change, In Edwards, M., & Fowler A. (Eds.), *The Earthscan Reader on NGO Management*. London: Earthscan.

Taylor, J. (2009) *Organizations – the Melting Pots of Social Change*. Retrieved from The Barefoot Guide to Working with Organizations and Social Change, www.barefootguide.

Ubels, J., Acquaye-Baddoo, N., & Fowler, A. (Eds.) (2010) *Capacity Development in Practice*. London: Earthscan Ltd.

UNDP (1998) *Capacity Assessment and Development, in a Systems and Strategic Management Context*. Technical Advisory Paper No 3. Retrieved from http://magnet.undp.org/Docs/cap/CAPTECH3. htm.

——, (2006) *Capacity Development Practice Note*. Retrieved November, 27, 2006, from *www*.capacity.undp.org/index.cfm?module=Library&page=Document&DocumentID=5599.

——, (2008) *Capacity Development Practice Note*. Retrieved May, 1, 2012, from www.capacity.undp.org/index.cfm?module=Library&page=Document&DocumentID=5599.

——, (2009) *Capacity Development: A UNDP Primer, UNDP Bureau for Development Policy*. Retrieved May, 5, 2012, from http://www.undp.org/content/undp/en/home/librarypage/capacity-building.html.

——, (2010) *Measuring Capacity, UNDP Capacity Development Group, Bureau for Development Policy*. Retrieved May, 5, 2012, from http://www.undp.org/content/undp/en/home/librarypage/capacity-building/undp-paper-on-measuring-capacity.html.

Van der Velden, F. (2002) Private Development Aid in Transition (Chapter 8). In Van der Velden, F., & Schulpen, L. *Private Development Aid in Transition* (p.150-154). New Delhi/India: Concept Publication Company.

——, (2004) *Capacity for Development: A Plea for a Real Paradigm Shift*. Contextual No. 2. Utrecht: Context, international cooperation (http://contextinternationalcooperation.files.wordpress.com/2007/12/contextuals-no-2.pdf).

Van der Velden, F., Esteves, P. & Joshi, V. (2005) *Where Action Speaks Louder Than Words; Report of the External Evaluation of the Core Programme of the Centre for Community Economics and Development Consultants Society*, Jaipur, Rajasthan, India.

Van der Velden, F., & Fernando, U. (2011) *Capacities for Development; Synthesis Report Joint Evaluation Partos Capacity Development*, final report. Amsterdam/Utrecht: Partos/Context, international cooperation.

Van der Velden, F. *et al.* (2008) *Organising Capacities for Societal Change; Experiences from South Africa.* Bonn/Utrecht: EED/Context, international cooperation.

Van der Velden, F., & Leenknegt, A.M. (2006) *Facilitation of Organisational Change: Beyond Organisational and Institutional Development.* Contextual No. 5. Utrecht: Context, international cooperation (http://contextinternationalcooperation.files.wordpress.com/2007/12/contextuals-no-5.pdf).

Van der Velden, F.; Leenknegt, A.; and Haijtink, A. (2005) *Capacity Development Services; A Learning Approach to Enhancing Capacity in SNV East Africa.* Nairobi; SNV East and Southern Africa.

Van der Velden, F. & Zweers, J. (1997) Personele samenwerking; Beleid, resultaten en perspectieven. In K. Lieten & F. van der Velden (Red.), *grenzen aan de hulp; beleid en effecten van ontwikkelingssamenwerking* (p. 245-269). Amsterdam: Uitgeverij Het Spinhuis.

Wheatley, M. (1999) *Leadership and the New Science; Discovering Order in A Chaotic World.* San Francisco: Berret-Koehler Pubishers.

Wigboldus, S. *et al.* (2011) *Critical Success Factors in Capacity Development Support: An Exploration in the Context of International Development Cooperation.* Wageningen: Wageningen UR Centre for Development Innovation.

Woodhill, J. (2010) *Capacities for Institutional Innovation: A Complexity Perspective.* IDS Bulletin, 41: 47–59.

Index